Looking to Christ: The Book of Hebrews

A Bible Study on Keeping the Faith When You Are Discouraged

MARCI OGROSKY

WESTBOW®
PRESS
A DIVISION OF THOMAS NELSON
& ZONDERVAN

Scripture quotations are from The Holy Bible, English Standard Version® (ESV®), copyright © 2001 by Crossway, a publishing ministry of Good News Publishers. Used by permission. All rights reserved.

WestBow Press books may be ordered through booksellers or by contacting:

WestBow Press
A Division of Thomas Nelson & Zondervan
1663 Liberty Drive
Bloomington, IN 47403
www.westbowpress.com
1 (866) 928-1240

Because of the dynamic nature of the Internet, any web addresses or links contained in this book may have changed since publication and may no longer be valid. The views expressed in this work are solely those of the author and do not necessarily reflect the views of the publisher, and the publisher hereby disclaims any responsibility for them.

Any people depicted in stock imagery provided by Thinkstock are models, and such images are being used for illustrative purposes only. Certain stock imagery © Thinkstock.

ISBN: 978-1-4908-3998-1 (sc)
ISBN: 978-1-4908-3999-8 (e)

Library of Congress Control Number: 2014910707

Printed in the United States of America.

WestBow Press rev. date: 07/24/2014

Contents

SECTION IV: PRACTICAL EVIDENCE OF OUR SALVATION

THE *Faith* TRILOGY

A BIBLE STUDY SERIES BY MARCI OGROSKY

❧ Time Line ❧

B.C. (Before Christ) or B.C.E. (Before the Common Era)		Adam & Eve (Creation)
		Noah (Flood)
	2000	Abraham (Patriarchs)
	1500	Moses (Exodus)
	1000	David (United Kingdom)
	500	Return from Exile
A.D. *(Anno Domini,* In the Year of Our Lord) or C.E. (the Common Era)	1	**JESUS CHRIST** Book of Hebrews
	500	Mohammed (Islam, 600s)
	1000	Catholic/Orthodox Split
	1500	Luther, Calvin (Reformation)
	2000	Us

❧ Introduction ❧

If you have ever been discouraged in your faith, the book of Hebrews is for you.

It really doesn't matter what has caused your discouragement. You might be facing ridicule, persecution, betrayal, illness, loss of relationship, hard circumstances, apathy, or nagging doubts about the truth of Christianity. Whatever the cause of your weakened faith, Hebrews is there to encourage you "so that you may not grow weary or fainthearted" (Hebrews 12:3 ESV).

How does the author of Hebrews accomplish this? He sets forth three essential ways for us to keep the faith:

1. Know who Jesus Christ is and what He has done.
2. Be inspired by others who have persevered in faith.
3. Live out your faith with enduring hope and brotherly love.

Notice that we are encouraged in our faith from three perspectives: God, others, and self. God has revealed the historical fact of the person and saving work of Jesus Christ. Other believers faithfully testify to the truth of God's salvation. It is also proved to us by our own experience in living out our faith. Therefore, we have assurance of faith based on facts, witnesses, and personal experience.

The author of Hebrews unpacks these perspectives with a passion and drive that leaves the reader breathless. This is a book filled with solid food for those who want to grow in spiritual maturity. There is a special emphasis in Hebrews on orthodoxy (right doctrine and thinking) that is carefully grounded in Scripture, and we are called to engage our mind, emotions, and behavior as we read and respond.

A unique feature of the book of Hebrews is its focus on Jesus' role as our high priest, a concept unfamiliar to many Christians today. God has ordained that we approach Him through the high priest of His choosing, Jesus Christ. Hebrews spends a great deal of time on this vital concept because what Jesus is doing for us in heaven right now is of eternal significance:

> "Consequently, he is able to save to the uttermost
> those who draw near to God through him, since he
> always lives to make intercession for them."
> (Hebrews 7:25)

We can be assured our faith in Jesus is grounded on rock solid reality even though His priestly intercession in heaven is invisible to us. We need this assurance more than ever in a relativistic culture where it is denied that truth or reality can be known. Believers are to persevere in faith to the end of life knowing for certain that their hope of salvation is securely anchored in the inner places of heaven where Christ pleads on their behalf:

> "We have this as a sure and steadfast anchor of the soul,
> a hope that enters into the inner place behind the curtain,
> where Jesus has gone as a forerunner on our behalf."
> (Hebrews 6:19-20)

> "Now faith is the assurance of things hoped for,
> the conviction of things not seen."
> (Hebrews 11:1)

The book of Hebrews fills us with confident hope of heaven, insight into salvation in Christ, a desire to worship Him, and love for others. No wonder it has been said that reading the book of Hebrews is like breathing the atmosphere of heaven itself. You are sure to be inspired by the Christology (study of the person and work of Jesus Christ) presented in Hebrews.

This study guide is designed for group or individual Bible study. The lessons provide background information, related Scripture references, and study questions to deepen the reader's understanding of the Bible passage along with its application to our lives. There are six sets of study questions per lesson, making it easier to study the lesson a little at a time during a week. A leader's guide and other appendices are provided near the end of the book.

The closing devotion for each lesson is adapted from the writings of Charles H. Spurgeon, one of the best-known preachers of all time. Spurgeon was a 19th century Baptist minister in England whose love for people and God's word was evident whenever he spoke. Crowds of thousands hungered to hear his message of hope and salvation in Jesus Christ. If you are not yet familiar with Spurgeon's warm and inspiring meditations, you are in for a treat.

Christians are meant to finish well. Scripture assures us that all true believers will spend eternity with our Lord and Savior, Jesus Christ. It is hoped that this study of the book of Hebrews will encourage you to grow more mature in your faith so that you persevere in confidence to the end of life. As you run with endurance the race set before you, may you be encouraged by constantly looking to Jesus Christ, the author and perfecter of our faith.

SECTION I

THE PERSON OF JESUS CHRIST

(WHO HE IS)

❧ Lesson 1 ❧

Christ's Divinity: The Son of God

Hebrews 1:1-4

Welcome to this study of the New Testament book of Hebrews. Before starting Lesson 1, please take about an hour to read all thirteen chapters of Hebrews to get an overview of the book. As you read, keep in mind that the overall purpose of Hebrews is to encourage Christians to keep the faith.

Part I: Setting the Stage

Purpose

This lesson explores the foundational truth that Jesus Christ is the Son of God, fully divine, fully God. It is important for us to acknowledge the deity of Christ because our salvation depends on His perfect and infinite divine nature.

Look for the following application points in this lesson:

1. The Son of God is fully divine, God Himself.
2. The Son of God is the second person of the Trinity.
3. Jesus Christ is the Son of God, fully divine, fully God.

Author of Hebrews

No one knows who wrote the book of Hebrews. The early church was divided as to whether the apostle Paul was the author, but the consensus today is that he was not. Perhaps the most compelling argument against Paul's authorship is that the author heard the gospel from the apostles (Hebrews 2:3), whereas Paul always claimed direct revelation from Christ. The author was a male who understood Old Testament ritual, wrote excellent Greek, and planned to travel with Timothy. Possible authors include Luke, Barnabas, Apollos, or Silas.

Date

It is presumed that Hebrews was written in the 1st century because Clement of Rome quotes it in his letter to the church in Corinth around A.D. 96. Hebrews was probably written before the destruction of the Temple in A.D. 70 as there seem to be references to sacrifices still being made (Hebrews 10:2-3, 11).

Literary Genre

Hebrews is considered a letter even though it lacks certain formatting such as a greeting. It is also an exhortation, warning readers not to weaken their faith by acting like unbelievers.

Audience

We do not know who the original audience was. A reasonable guess is that the author lived in Judea and the recipients were Hellenistic (Greek-speaking) Jewish Christians in Rome. It seems that the letter was meant to be shared among house churches. The author sends greetings on behalf of "those from Italy" (Hebrews 13:24), perhaps Jewish Christians who fled Rome under Claudius' edict of eviction in A.D. 49.

Theme

The main theme of Hebrews is encouragement to keep the faith based on the perfect and final sacrifice and high priesthood of Jesus Christ. We can have utmost confidence in Christ's atoning work and ongoing intercession.

Title

All early manuscripts bear the title Hebrews but the word does not appear in the letter itself, making it unknown whether the author chose it. It may be a reference to the time from Abraham to Moses when Jews were known as Hebrews, a period frequently cited in the letter. The title may have reminded Jewish Christians not to cling to the old Mosaic covenant, for true descendants of Abraham are to live in the new covenant in Christ.[1]

Outline of Hebrews

There are several good ways to outline the book of Hebrews. Below is a simple outline that summarizes three ways for us to keep the faith.

Outline of Hebrews

Part II: Studying Scripture

Ancient letters normally began with a greeting just like today. However, the author of Hebrews dives into his message without any salutation and creates a sense of urgency that grabs our attention. Within a few verses he states enough doctrine about the person and work of Jesus Christ to fill volumes of exposition. Clearly this is no ordinary letter.

Read Hebrews 1:1-4

1. The Fulfillment of Revelation

God delights to make Himself known to us. He has revealed Himself in two ages of self-revelation, the Old Testament era and New Testament era. There is continuity between the two eras of revelation, but this passage also points out some important differences summarized in the chart below.

God's Revelation

	Old Testament Era (v. 1)	New Testament Era (v. 2)
When?	Long ago, in the past	These last days
How?	Many times, many ways	One time; in full *(implied)*
To whom?	Our forefathers	Us
By whom?	Many human prophets	God's one divine Son

a) In the Old Testament era God made His word known to prophets throughout the centuries by means of visions, dreams, and direct speech. Why do you think it was necessary for God to reveal Himself to the prophets in many limited times and ways rather than all at once in full?

b) The last messianic prophecy of the Old Testament was from Malachi four hundred years before Christ. God's lengthy silence after Malachi implied there was no need for Him to reveal anything more about His promises until the time of fulfillment. How patient are you when it comes to waiting for God to act on His promises? How can you learn to respond to God's silence with eager anticipation rather than discouragement?

c) Christ's first coming ushered in the period of time the author of Hebrews calls the last or latter days. The last days have continued for two thousand years and will continue until Christ returns. That means we currently live in the last days. Looking at the above chart, why is the present era of revelation in these last days superior to revelation in the Old Testament era?

2. The Son Is Fully Divine, Fully God

The author starts his letter by laying down a foundational understanding of who the Son of God is. The Son is a divine person distinct from the Father (an exact imprint), and yet He is one being with the Father, fully God (the radiance of His glory). In v. 2-3, we see hints of the fullness of the Son's deity. What brief details do we learn about each aspect of His divinity?

v. 2　　Prophet:　　_____

　　　　Heir:　　　_____

　　　　Creator:　　_____

v. 3　　Essence of God:　_____

　　　　　　　　　　_____

　　　　Upholder:　　_____

　　　　Priest:　　　_____

　　　　King:　　　　_____

3. The Son of God and the Trinity

The Son of God is a distinct person from God the Father and God the Holy Spirit. These three persons are each fully God and yet together they are one God. This is monotheism (belief in one god), not polytheism (belief in many gods). A traditional definition of the mystery of the Trinity is:

> God (also called the Godhead or Trinity) is one Being revealed in three persons, Father, Son, and Holy Spirit.

The Dutch theologian Herman Bavinck sums up the importance of the doctrine of the Trinity:

> "The entire Christian belief system, all of special revelation, stands or falls with the confession of God's Trinity. It is the core of the Christian faith, the root of all its dogmas, the basic content of the new covenant."[2]

a) People use various analogies to explain the Trinity and each one is helpful to an extent, but in the end they all miss some aspect of the Trinity.[3] For example, how is a three-leaf shamrock a good analogy of the Trinity? Or an egg with yolk, white and shell? Yet what do these analogies fail to convey about the *fullness* of each person of the Trinity?

b) Other analogies may inadvertently teach modalism, a heresy (unorthodox belief) that says God is one Being or Person who acts at different times in different modes or roles as Father, Son, and Holy Spirit. One example is a person who acts as a lawyer, neighbor, or parent in different situations. Or water that takes the form of either ice, liquid, or steam at different times. As helpful as these analogies might be, what do they fail to convey about the plurality of the Trinity, or the *distinctness* of each person of the Trinity?

c) The word Trinity (meaning "tri-unity") is not in the Bible, but the concept of a triune or three-in-one God definitely is. For instance, how are all three persons of the Trinity evident at Jesus' baptism? (See Matthew 3:16-17)

4. The Son's Two Natures

The Son is always identified as the second person of the Trinity. The Son, as we will see in Hebrews, is Jesus of Nazareth who is both fully human and fully divine. A carefully worded traditional definition worked out by theologians over the centuries is:

> *Jesus Christ, Son of God, is one Person with two natures, divine and human.*

a) Unfortunately, confusion about Jesus Christ's two natures has led to numerous heresies. Devaluing Christ's *divinity* is associated with moralism, Arianism, and Deism.[4] If you had a friend who said Scripture portrays Jesus only as a good, moral human, how would you use v. 2-3 to explain that Scripture also portrays Him as divine?

b) Devaluing Jesus' *humanity* is associated with pantheism and Gnosticism.[5] Why do you think it was necessary for Jesus to have a human body of flesh and blood in order to secure our salvation? We will spend more time on Jesus' human nature in Lessons 3 and 4.

c) Which of Christ's natures do you think is most devalued today, His divinity or humanity? Why do you think this is so? What can we do to keep in mind the full picture of who He is?

5. Superior to Angels

In v. 4, the author insists that the Son is superior to angels. This is a significant claim. Since angels are the highest spirit beings in the universe apart from the Godhead, anyone higher than angels would be on the same level with God Himself.

Angels are created spirits who are immortal and far superior to humans in power, ability and knowledge. Jewish tradition held angels in high regard because they were associated with God's redemption in the Exodus (Exodus 3:2) and God's revelation of the Law to Moses at Mount Sinai (Deuteronomy 33:2; Acts 7:53). Anyone more excellent than angels would have to be more closely associated with God's redemptive and revelatory work than angels.

a) In v. 3, which aspect of the Son's divinity indicates to you that, unlike angels, He reveals God perfectly?

b) Again in v. 3, which aspect of the Son's divinity indicates to you that He accomplishes our redemption perfectly?

6. An Excellent Name

a) In v. 4, the author speaks of an inherited name that is more excellent than the name angel (meaning "messenger of God"). The inherited name that surpasses angels cannot here be the human name Jesus since that name does not appear in this chapter and does not reflect the relationship of an heir. What, then, is the excellent inherited name, stated in v. 2?

b) Why do you think it is more excellent to be an heir (Son) than a servant (angel)?

c) The author is making the case that the Son is divine and is in fact God Himself. Whoever is the Son of God is God, not an angelic being or a semi-God. Read v. 1-4 again and linger over each aspect of the Son's deity, praying for the Holy Spirit to broaden and deepen your understanding of who God's beloved Son, Jesus Christ, truly is.

Part III: Personal Application and Growth

If you feel a bit overwhelmed by the material in this lesson, you are not alone. Two of the deepest mysteries in Christianity are the Trinity (one Being revealed in three persons) and the person of Jesus Christ (two natures united in one person). These concepts are foundational to our faith.

Today's lesson points to several important truths that apply to our personal lives. Allow these truths to penetrate your mind, soften your heart, deepen your faith and affect your behavior to help you continually grow in Christ.

1.   The Son of God is fully divine, God Himself.

Considering the author's purpose of encouragement to keep the faith, we should note that he wisely begins with an emphasis on the Son's divinity rather than the Son's humanity. When people begin with Jesus' humanity they often develop an unbiblical view that Jesus was a mere man aspiring to be God, a view that makes them resent or resist Jesus. We need to remember that *Christ was God before He was man.* Make up a phrase of your own to help you remember this concept.

2.   The Son of God is the second person of the Trinity.

The concept of the Trinity is frequently misunderstood. We should stay close to the traditional definition worked out by early theologians: God (the Godhead) is one Being revealed in three persons, Father (the first person), Son (the second person), and Holy Spirit (the third person). Relying on this definition, how would you answer someone who wrongly accuses Christians of worshiping three gods?

3.   Jesus Christ is the Son of God, fully divine, fully God.

Theologian Abraham Kuyper gives us these memorable words about the deity of Christ:

> "There is not a square inch in the whole domain of our human existence, over which Christ, who is sovereign over all, does not cry, 'Mine!'"[6]

This week try to look at every square inch of Creation as belonging to Christ: the sky, stars, ground, plants, animals, people's emotions, bodies, and intellect. In what ways will this outlook deepen your understanding of Christ the King and Upholder of the universe?

Part IV: Closing Devotion

by Charles Spurgeon

Believer, there is a fullness in Christ. There is a fullness of essential Deity, for "in him the whole fullness of deity dwells bodily" (Colossians 2:9).

There is a fullness of blessings of every sort and shape: a fullness of grace to pardon, to regenerate, to sanctify, to preserve, and to perfect. There is a fullness at all times: a fullness of comfort in affliction and guidance in prosperity. There is a fullness of every divine attribute: of wisdom, of power, of love.

There is a fullness which is impossible to survey, much less to explore. Fullness, indeed, must there be when the stream is always flowing and the well springs up as free, as rich, as full as ever.

Come, believer, and get all your need supplied; ask largely and you will receive largely, for this fullness is inexhaustible, and is treasured up where all the needy may reach it, in Jesus, Immanuel – God with us.[7]

❧ Lesson 2 ❧

Christ's Divinity: The Messiah

Hebrews 1:5-14

Part I: Setting the Stage

Purpose

This lesson continues to explore the foundational truth that Jesus Christ is fully divine, fully God. The author offers seven proof texts from the Old Testament to validate his claims. It is important for us to realize that God foretold that the promised human Messiah was also to be the divine Son of God, fully God, far superior to angels in His nature and status.

Look for the following application points in this lesson:

1. Jesus is the promised Messiah, the Son of God, God Himself.
2. Jesus is superior to angels and enthroned at God's right hand.
3. Angels are created spirit beings who, like us, worship God the Son, Jesus Christ.

The Messiah, Son of God

God promised over the centuries that He would send a Messiah (*masiah* in Hebrew, meaning "anointed one") to save His people. Some of these prophecies are recorded in the messianic psalms and others are found in the writings of the prophets and elsewhere. Hints of messianic prophecy can be traced back to Genesis 3:15 where God promised to ultimately defeat Satan through Adam and Eve's offspring, the Messiah.

By the time of Jesus' birth the Jews tended to think of the coming Messiah in terms of a political and military leader who would restore national Israel to her former days of glory. People had to be reminded that Scripture also spoke of the Messiah as a suffering servant who would die to save God's people. Upon his death the Messiah would be enthroned in heaven at God's right hand as the Son of God, God Himself.

The Hebrew word *masiah* is translated *christos* in Greek. Therefore, the title Jesus Christ is equivalent to Jesus the Messiah or Jesus the Anointed One. Another title for the Messiah is Son of God, emphasizing His divinity. This is the title the apostles used for Jesus. Jesus preferred to refer to Himself by the messianic title Son of Man. Still another title was Son of David, pointing to the Messiah's permanent reign on David's throne.

Jesus Christ's Divine Nature

Christ's divine nature is from all eternity. When He took on a human nature and lived on earth, Christ sometimes acted in ways that emphasized His divine nature. For example, He performed miracles that divinely interrupted natural laws. He walked on water, multiplied food, raised people from death, healed, changed water to wine, calmed a storm, made the blind see and the lame walk.

Further, in His divine nature Christ had knowledge of things no mere human could know. When He forgave the sins of a paralytic man, He knew the silent accusations the scribes were making against Him in their hearts (Mark 2:6-8). Christ knew from the beginning which followers would be unbelievers and which one would betray Him (John 6:64).

Old Testament Proof Texts

The author supports his assertions about the Son's deity with a chain of seven quotations from the Old Testament. The Old Testament or Hebrew Bible is known to Jews as the Mikra ("that which is read") or Tanakh. Tanakh is an acronym of three consonants (TNK) that stand for the three parts of the Hebrew Bible: Torah (Law), Naviim (Prophets), and Ketuvim (Writings).

Jesus said all three parts of Scripture testify to Him (Luke 24:27, 44). The author of Hebrews appropriately chooses proof texts that represent the entire Hebrew Bible: Deuteronomy (Law), Second Samuel (Prophets), and the Psalms (Writings), beginning and ending with messianic psalms.

It should be pointed out that we will not always find the author's exact wording of these proof texts when we look them up in our Old Testament. Our Old Testament is based on Hebrew manuscripts called the Masoretic Text. However, the author of Hebrews often relies on a different version of the Old Testament called the Septuagint. The Septuagint is an ancient Greek translation based in part on Hebrew manuscripts not known to us today.

Whether proof texts are from the Septuagint or the Masoretic Text, we will benefit from considering their original context. Then we can better appreciate why the author of Hebrews chose these particular passages to verify that the Messiah is the divine Son of God, God Himself. Allow the consistent testimony of God's word over the ages to encourage you to hold fast to your faith.

Part II: Studying Scripture

The previous lesson looked at the opening paragraph of Hebrews where seven aspects of the Son's divinity were listed. The Son is the *heir* and the very *essence* of God; the *creator* and *upholder* of the universe; and the perfect fulfillment of *prophet*, *priest*, and *king*.

Now the author supports his statements with seven proof texts from the Old Testament, some written a thousand years earlier. Together the proof texts validate the Son's deity, affirming that the Messiah is the enthroned Son of God, God Himself, far superior to angels.

Read Hebrews 1:5-14

1. The Son's Relationship to the Father

a) Read Psalm 2:6-8, the first proof text. This messianic psalm speaks of God exalting His king over all earthly kings. The Messiah is God's exalted king to whom God says,

> "You are my Son, today I have begotten you."
> (Hebrews 1:5a)

The term begotten has a couple of meanings with regard to the divine Son. First, begotten tells us the Son is of the Father, not a created being like humans or angels. Second, begotten means established. God raised and established His Son on the throne when the Son's saving work on the cross was completed. The proof text could mean that God enthroned His Son on a certain day in history, or it could mean that the Messiah became His Son on the day of enthronement.

What is your answer to the question about angels in Hebrews 1:5a? Why?

b) Read II Samuel 7:12-16, the second proof text. God promises to establish David's throne forever and be a father to the king, ensuring his inheritance. The author of Hebrews treats this passage as messianic. God says of the Messiah to be enthroned,

> "I will be to him a father and he shall be to me a son."
> (Hebrews 1:5b)

In v. 5b, what point does the author make in common with v. 5a?

c) In your opinion, which aspect(s) of the Son's divinity is supported by this pair of proof texts?

2. The Son's Relationship to Angels

a) The third proof text is from a messianic portion of the Song of Moses where angels praise God for His reign over the world (Deuteronomy 32:43, Septuagint version). As used in the book of Hebrews, God redirects heaven's worship to the Messiah, the incarnate Son who is firstborn or pre-eminent. God declares that the praise due to God should go to the Son:

> "Let all God's angels worship him."
> (Hebrews 1:6)

What actions and words do you imagine angels employ in worshiping the Son? Which of these elements could you incorporate more fully into your worship?

b) The fourth proof text comes from a nature psalm praising God the Creator (Psalm 104:4, Septuagint version). Psalm 104 was not known as a messianic psalm but becomes one in the book of Hebrews where God redirects His people's praise to the Messiah, His Son, the Creator who commands the angels:

> "He makes his angels winds,
> and his ministers a flame of fire."
> (Hebrews 1:7)

Notice the metaphor of storm imagery in this poetic couplet. What type of fire occurs in a storm? How does it comfort you to know the Son controls nature?

c) In your opinion, which aspect(s) of the Son's divinity is supported by this pair of proof texts?

3. The Son Is God

a) Read Psalm 45:6-7, the fifth proof text. Psalm 45 was written for a royal wedding and praises the king's lasting reign of righteousness. This passage takes on messianic meaning in Hebrews where God says to the Messiah, His Son, that the Son is God and the Son's righteous reign will have no end:

> "Your throne, O God (*theos*), is forever and ever..."
> (Hebrews 1:8-9)

Theos is the Greek equivalent of *Elohim*, the Hebrew word for God. It is highly significant that God addresses His Son as God. Explain how you would use this text to assure a new believer that the Son is truly God.

b) The sixth proof text praises God's unchangeableness (Psalm 102:25-27, Septuagint version). God is the eternal, unchanging Creator, whereas the Creation will wear out like a garment. Psalm 102 was not known as a messianic psalm but is treated like one in Hebrews where the praise due to God is redirected by God to the Messiah, His Son. God calls His Son Lord, the same title that belongs to God Himself:

> "You, Lord (*kyrios*), laid the foundation of the earth in the
> beginning, and the heavens are the work of your hands;
> they will perish, but you remain..."
> (Hebrews 1:10-12)

How does it make you feel to know that God's character and plan of salvation are unchangeable?

c) In your opinion, which aspect(s) of the Son's divinity is supported by this pair of proof texts?

4. The Son Is Victorious

a) Read Psalm 110:1, the seventh and last proof text. This messianic psalm was originally written for a king's coronation. In the book of Hebrews, God (LORD) says to the king (Lord), who is the Messiah,

> "Sit at my right hand until I make your
> enemies a footstool for your feet."
> (Hebrews 1:13)

This is the most frequently quoted Old Testament passage in the New Testament. Its use here brings us to the climax of the chapter. Believers can have confidence and strength to endure in faith because God sees to it that the Messiah reigns victorious over His enemies. In your opinion, which aspect(s) of the Son's divinity is supported by this proof text?

b) The chapter ends with a statement that echoes two psalms (Psalm 34:7 and Psalm 91:11). In v. 14, how does the Messiah use His position of authority for the benefit of believers? In your opinion, which aspect(s) of the Son's divinity does this verse support? What should be our response to the fact that the Son safeguards our inheritance of salvation?

c) Read Romans 8:16-17. What further means of assurance is given so that we might know we belong to God and will inherit salvation in Christ?

5. Our Response to the Son

In v. 5 and 13, the author begins and ends the chain of proof texts with two messianic psalms introduced by the same rhetorical question, "To which of the angels did God ever say...?" This forms an *inclusio* or enclosure around the proof texts to make them stand out. The point is not only that the Messiah is superior to angels, but the Messiah is the Messianic King, Son of God, and God. The chart below summarizes v. 5-13 in light of their proof texts.

The Messiah Is the Enthroned Son of God, God Himself

<u>Verse</u>   <u>Summary and Proof Text</u>

1:5a   No angel is the begotten or enthroned Son of God (Ps. 2:6-8).

1:5b   God is the Son's father; angels are not God's heirs (II Sam. 7:12-16).

1:6   Angels worship the pre-eminent Son who is God (Deut. 32:43).

1:7   The Son created angels to serve Him mightily (Ps. 104:4).

1:8-9   The Son is God and a righteous King forever (Ps. 45:6-7).

1:10-12   The Son is the eternal, unchangeable Lord and Creator (Ps. 102:25-27).

1:13   God ensures that the Messiah, His Son, is enthroned (Ps. 110:1).

---

a)   Looking at the above chart, what have you learned about the Son in this lesson? How will your prayers and worship reflect your new insight?

b)   Read Colossians 1:15-20 where the apostle Paul affirms Christ's deity. Find at least three essential concepts there about the Son that remind you of the first chapter of Hebrews.

c)   Read John 1:1-5, 14, 18, and 20:28-29. Summarize briefly what the apostle John says with regard to Christ's deity. What is your response to Scripture's consistent testimony about the divinity of Christ?

6.   Why Jesus Has to Be Divine to Save Us

Scripture teaches us that belief in the deity of Jesus Christ is essential for Christians. Take time to meditate on the following five reasons why the Son's divinity is necessary for our salvation. Which two are most important to you? Commit those to memory in order to encourage yourself and others.

1)   Only an infinite being could bear the penalty for all the world's sin.
2)   Only a sinless being could obey God perfectly.
3)   Only God can save.
4)   Only God can mediate perfectly between Himself and humans.
5)   No mere sinful human can intercede for us in God's holy presence.

Part III: Personal Application and Growth

Today's lesson points to several important truths that apply to our personal lives. Allow these truths to penetrate your mind, soften your heart, deepen your faith and affect your behavior to help you continually grow in Christ.

1.   Jesus is the promised Messiah, the Son of God, God Himself.

There is an unfortunate trend in modern Christianity to deny the deity of Christ. In some mainline denominations pastors are no longer required to affirm Christ's deity in order to be ordained. If someone in your church questions whether Jesus is really God, what specific verses from Hebrews 1 will you share to reassure him or her that Scripture teaches the divinity of Christ?

2.   Jesus is superior to angels and enthroned at God's right hand.

This week find a hymn or song that praises Jesus as King and try to learn the words. Perhaps start with the praise song, "Majesty, Worship His Majesty."[8] How will you benefit from filling your heart with praises to Jesus our King?

3. Angels are created spirit beings who, like us, worship God the Son, Jesus Christ.

The historic Belgic Confession, Article 10, speaks of Jesus' divinity:

> "We believe that Jesus Christ, according to his divine nature, is the only Son of God... He is the Son of God not only from the time he assumed our nature but from all eternity...So then, he is the true eternal God, the Almighty, whom we invoke, worship, and serve."[9]

In what ways will you invoke, worship and serve Jesus Christ today?

Part IV: Closing Devotion
by Charles Spurgeon

Believer, delight in serving the divine. Our God is the Lord of the empire of love and would have His servants dressed in the livery of joy. The angels of God serve Him with songs, not with groans; a murmur or a sigh would be a mutiny in their ranks. Service coupled with cheerfulness is heart-service, and therefore true.

Take away joyful willingness from the Christian and you have removed the *evidence of sincerity.* Cheerfulness is the *support of our strength*; in the joy of the Lord are we strong. It acts as the *remover of difficulties.* Cheerfulness is to our service what oil is to the wheels of a railway carriage. Without oil the axle soon grows hot and accidents occur; and if there be not a holy cheerfulness to oil our wheels, our spirits will be clogged with weariness.

Believer, let us put this question – do you serve Christ the Lord with gladness? Let us show to the people of the world that it is to us a delight and a joy! Let our gladness proclaim that we serve a good Master.[10]

❧ Lesson 3 ❧

Jesus' Humanity: Our Savior

Hebrews 2:1-9

Part I: Setting the Stage

Purpose

This lesson brings us to another foundational truth about the person of Jesus Christ. He is fully human, God incarnate (in the flesh). It is important for us to understand that Jesus' humanity was necessary in order for Him to suffer and die in our place to save us.

Look for the following application points in this lesson:

1. Jesus Christ is fully human, God incarnate.
2. Jesus restored humanity's divinely ordained role as ruler of creation.
3. Jesus had to suffer and die in our place in order to be our Savior.

Human Like Us

Having addressed the Son's divinity in the first chapter, the author now turns his attention to the Son's human nature. In some ways this will be easier for us to comprehend because we have experience in being human. We know what it means for Jesus to be flesh and blood. By sharing in our humanity He felt the limitations of weakness, temptation, and pain. Jesus is able to sympathize with our human condition.

Scripture records many instances that emphasize Jesus' human nature. For example, He was able to eat, drink, sleep, sit, walk, become weak, read, sing, ride a donkey, bleed, and die. He learned, felt sorrow, wept, prayed, and was tempted, although He never sinned.

Further, in His human nature there were things He did not know. We can all identify with that. Jesus did not know the day or hour when a major event would occur (Mark 13:32). When a woman in a crowd was healed after touching His garment, Jesus felt the power go out but apparently did not know who touched Him (Luke 8:45-47).

Perfect Obedience

Jesus was made human in every respect except He was without a human father and without sin. He did not inherit His human mother Mary's sinful nature, evidently due to the protection of the Holy Spirit. However, His sinlessness did not prevent Him from facing the limitations and struggles of life as a finite human. He is able to identify with our weakness because He became human.

We might ask whether it was possible for Jesus to have sinned when tempted. The issue is not explicitly addressed in Scripture, but it seems that the short answer must be no, it was not possible for Jesus to sin. Theologians arrive at this conclusion by various paths. When we pursue some of these complicated paths we soon find ourselves ready to agree with theologian Geerhardus Vos, "We simply must confess our inability to throw light upon it."[11]

Some people wonder whether Jesus was truly tempted, knowing He could not yield to sin. The short answer is yes, in His humanity Jesus suffered temptation just like us. Once again we find that the issue is complicated. Jesus somehow refused to rely on His divine nature to make obedience easier. He rendered perfect obedience in His humanity by relying perfectly on God the Father and God the Holy Spirit, thereby accomplishing what Adam had failed to do.

The Union of Jesus' Divine and Human Natures

It is a profound mystery that Jesus' human and divine natures are forever united in His person and yet remain distinct. His human nature was never absorbed into His divine nature, and His divine nature was never forfeited.

Theologians use a technical term, "the hypostatic union," to describe the mystery of the union of Jesus' two natures in His person. No one can explain exactly how the hypostatic union works since there is nothing else like it. The person of Jesus is unique. Since the permanent union of Jesus' two natures is essential for our salvation, it is a reason for our continual praise.

Theologian Wayne Grudem comments on Scripture's evidence that the divine Son of God became human forever:

> "All of these texts indicate that Jesus did not *temporarily* become man, but that his divine nature was *permanently* united to his human nature, and he lives forever not just as the eternal Son of God, the second person of the Trinity, but also as Jesus, the man who was born of Mary, and as Christ, the Messiah and Savior of his people. Jesus will remain fully God and fully man, yet one person, forever."[12]

Part II: Studying Scripture

Read Hebrews 2:1-4

1. Pay Closer Attention

In the first chapter of Hebrews the author contrasted revelation of God by the prophets to the superior revelation by the divine Son. Now in the author's orderly way he contrasts revelation of God by angels to the superior revelation by the human Jesus, summarized in the chart below.

God's Revelation

	Old Testament Era (v. 2)	New Testament Era (v. 3)
Revelation?	Law; old covenant *(implied)*	Salvation; new covenant
Declared by?	Angels	Lord Jesus
If we reject it?	Retribution, punishment	Eternal judgment *(implied)*

---

a) Here we have the first of several warnings in Hebrews to pay attention. The word "therefore" links this chapter to chapter 1. Because of what we know about the Son's deity, we should pay particular attention to what He revealed when He came as a human. Looking at the above chart, what superior revelation did Jesus declare?

b) In v. 1, the author cautions his readers not to "drift away," meaning they must not backslide, act like unbelievers, or adopt a careless attitude toward the things of God. In Hebrews drifting is not as dire as falling away into apostasy (the permanent rejection of God), but drifting can result in immature faith that cannot stand up to persecution. What are some reasons we drift away from God's word? Name some practical ways we can prevent drifting.

c) In v. 2, the "message declared by angels" was God's word revealed in the Mosaic Law at Mount Sinai (Acts 7:53). God's word was reliable and binding, and every violation of His word was an evil affront to God. What was the consequence of disobeying God's word, the Law?

2. The Gift of Salvation

a) The author argues from the lesser to the greater, reasoning that the more valuable the gift, the greater the penalty for rejecting it. If people were punished for rejecting the Law, then they will certainly face worse judgment for rejecting salvation, a gift greater than the Law. In v. 2-3a, how would you answer the rhetorical question about escaping retribution?

b) The word "escape" reminds us that the non-Christian life is a life of continual bondage to sin. Salvation in Christ is God's one and only plan for deliverance. Why do you think so many people try to devise an alternative plan instead of accepting God's salvation in Christ?

3. Witnesses to Salvation

a) In v. 3-4, how did the following persons verify the truth that salvation in Christ is a great revelation worthy of our closer attention?

God the Son ("the Lord"): _____

Apostles ("those who heard"): _____

God the Father: _____

God the Holy Spirit: _____

b) The Godhead is the essence of truth and the highest possible authority of truth. Why is it futile for anyone to seek more authoritative evidence for the truth of the gospel than already provided in Scripture by the testimony of the Father, Son, and Holy Spirit?

c) In v. 3b, from whom did the apostles learn about God's plan of salvation? From whom did the author of Hebrews learn it?

d) The apostolic testimony recorded in Scripture is where we learn who Jesus is and what He has done. With this in mind, why is it illogical for people to say they think Jesus was basically a good teacher but they don't believe in the Bible?

4.   God's Testimony

Verse 4 tells us God used miracles as a way to testify to salvation in Jesus. Biblical miracles were God's intervention into the ordinary course of nature for the purpose of authenticating the messenger and/or message as sent from God. The ultimate miracle proving the truth of the gospel was the resurrection.

Interestingly, there is no word for miracle in ancient Greek. In our English Bibles the word miracle translates the Greek words *dynamis* (power or mighty works), *teras* (wonders), *semeion* (sign), *ergon* (work), and *thauma* (marvels). In v. 4, the word "miracles" is literally "power" (*dynamis*).

In general, power and work refer to God's ability to perform a miracle, such as when Jesus healed a paralytic (Luke 5:17). Wonders and marvels elicit a response from the observer, usually a response of awe (Acts 2:43). Signs point to God's authority and reveal who Jesus is, as when Jesus changed water into wine (John 2:11).

a)   Since God used miracles to testify about Jesus, why is it spiritually dangerous for people to dismiss miracles as myths or try to discredit them by explaining them away with naturalistic explanations?

b)   Courtroom journalist Lee Strobel finds the apostles' eyewitness testimony to be powerful evidence for the truth of Christ's resurrection:

> "While most people can only have faith that their beliefs are true, the disciples were in a position to know without a doubt whether or not Jesus had risen from the dead. They claimed that they saw him, talked with him, and ate with him. If they weren't absolutely certain, they wouldn't have allowed themselves to be tortured to death for proclaiming that the Resurrection had happened."[13]

Why is it significant that there were hundreds of eyewitnesses to the resurrected Christ and that His appearances occurred over several weeks in different places?

c) In v. 4, God also testified about Jesus by means of the Holy Spirit's gifts. This is not the usual word for gifts (*charismata*), but a word meaning distributions (*merismoi*). It is a word unique to Hebrews, emphasizing the widespread and diverse nature of the Spirit's work. Why do you think God chose to testify about Jesus through the wide distribution of spiritual gifts? (See I Corinthians 12:4-11 and Romans 12:6-8 for lists of gifts.)

Read Hebrews 2:5-9

5. A Proof Text

In the first chapter the author gave seven Old Testament proof texts to support his claims about Christ's deity. Now he gives the first of four proof texts regarding Christ's humanity. The quote is from Psalm 8:4-6, a familiar psalm to the readers. This was not a messianic psalm but instead speaks of God's design for mankind to rule over creation.

Remember there are two meanings for the term "son of man." When capitalized in our Bibles, Son of Man is a messianic title that Jesus often used for Himself in the gospels. When the term son of man is not capitalized it normally means a human being.

a) In v. 5, the "world to come" refers to the last days, the time between Christ's two comings. We are now in the world to come, the last days. Who was *not* chosen to rule the world for God now or ever, in spite of their knowledge and power?

b) In v. 6-8, the pronouns "you" and "he" refer to God, while "him" and "his" likely refer to humanity. Re-read these verses substituting the words God and humanity in the appropriate places. Who was created to rule the world for God? (See also Genesis 1:28).

c) What do you think has gone wrong with that plan?

d) In v. 9, the pronouns "him" and "he" refer to Jesus. Jesus restores and fulfills the human destiny of ruling the world. How did Jesus become the crowned ruler of the world?

e) Why do you think the author introduces the human name Jesus in chapter 2 rather than in chapter 1?

6. Beneficiaries of Salvation

a) In v. 9, Jesus redeemed or tasted death for "everyone," meaning everyone God chooses for salvation. Jesus redeems and sanctifies only believers, not those outside His true church. What does that imply for unbelievers who permanently reject God?

b) Scripture does not teach universalism or the belief that everyone in the world is saved to eternal life. Looking ahead in v. 10, what phrase confirms that Jesus does not redeem everyone in the world?

c) Looking ahead in v. 13b, what phrase indicates that Jesus redeems only those whom God has chosen?

d) Read John 6:37-40. Who does Jesus say will come to Him? What will inevitably happen to those who come to Him? Let this be a source of great encouragement to you.

Part III: Personal Application and Growth

Today's lesson points to several important truths that apply to our personal lives. Allow these truths to penetrate your mind, soften your heart, deepen your faith and affect your behavior to help you continually grow in Christ.

1. Jesus Christ is fully human, God incarnate.

Jesus Christ's time on earth is called His humiliation. It includes His incarnation, suffering, death, burial, and descent into hell.[14] Each day this week take time to meditate on one of these aspects of Christ's humiliation. In what ways do you expect your meditations to help you appreciate more fully what Christ went through for you?

2. Jesus restored humanity's divinely ordained role as ruler of creation.

Believers are destined to co-reign with Christ one day. In preparation for ruling with Christ, what attitude will you begin to change this week so that you learn to love people more like our Lord Jesus Christ does?

3.   Jesus had to suffer and die in our place in order to be our Savior.

Our sins against God amount to cosmic treason, but Christ has already paid the death penalty we deserve. How will you express your gratitude to God today for what Christ has done for you? What practical difference will your gratitude make in the way you approach your everyday life?

Part IV: Closing Devotion

by Charles Spurgeon

Believer, why did Jesus allow Himself to be enrolled among sinners?

By this wonderful condescension He could better become their advocate. Now, when the sinner is brought to the bar, Jesus appears there Himself. He stands to answer the accusation. He points to His side, hands, and feet, and challenges Justice to bring anything against the sinners He represents. He pleads His blood so triumphantly that the Judge proclaims, "Let them go their way; deliver them from going down into the pit, for He has found a ransom."

Our Lord Jesus was holy; we were guilty. He transfers His name from the list of the holy to this guilty indictment, and our names are taken from the indictment and written in the roll of acceptance, for there is a complete transfer made between Jesus and His people. All our estate of misery and sin Jesus has taken; and all that Jesus has comes to us.

Rejoice, believer, in your union to Him who was numbered among the transgressors; and prove that you are truly saved by being manifestly numbered with those who are new creatures in Him.[15]

❧ Lesson 4 ❧

Jesus' Humanity: Our Brother

Hebrews 2:10-18

Part I: Setting the Stage

Purpose

This lesson reminds us that in His human nature Jesus faced the same kinds of temptations that we do. He overcame temptation by His perfect obedience to God and will help us overcome. Jesus understands and sympathizes with human weakness and therefore is a most merciful high priest for believers, His spiritual brothers and sisters. It is important for us to affirm the full humanity of Jesus Christ just as we need to affirm His full divinity.

Look for the following application points in this lesson:

1. Jesus suffered temptation and will help us when we are tempted.
2. Jesus is our sympathetic high priest when we fail to resist temptation.
3. Believers are spiritual brothers and sisters to Jesus and to each other.

One Big Family

Jesus said the believers were given to Him by God the Father. He called believers His brothers, a term that includes sisters, and so we have the privilege of calling Jesus our brother in return. Of course, Jesus is stronger, smarter, truer, more faithful, protective, and loving than any earthly brother we could ever have. Whether your experience with brothers has been positive, negative, or non-existent, Jesus is the ideal older brother surpassing all others.

Since we are Christ's brothers and sisters, we are also related to each other. This means all true believers in all eras of time belong to God's family, the universal church. It is a great comfort to discover that the body of Christ is a vast extended family that transcends blood relationships, time and space.

In this lifetime the local church is where we experience the delights as well as the frustrations of living and loving each other as precious brothers and sisters in Christ. After death we will be glorified and our relationships will be perfected.

Facing Temptation

Our brother Jesus understands what it is to suffer temptation. Temptation may be defined as being enticed to get what we want by doing something wrong. At the beginning of His ministry Jesus was tempted by Satan in the wilderness to misuse His role as the Son of God (Luke 4:1-13). If Jesus had given in, He would not have accomplished the perfect obedience to God necessary to secure our salvation. Jesus faced temptation in three main areas:

- Discontentment (judging God's provision of food to be inadequate)
- Idolatry (worshiping someone other than God for gain)
- Unbelief (failing to trust God's saving promises)

Jesus faced the same kinds of temptation in the wilderness the Israelites faced 1,500 years earlier.[16] The Israelites responded to temptation by complaining against God, turning to other gods, and failing to believe that God would save them. Unlike the Israelites, Jesus trusted God's provision, worshiped only God, and believed God's word without needing further proof.

Jesus' perfect obedience accomplished what the Israelites failed to do. Today when we face temptation we are to try to follow Jesus' example.

The Necessity of Jesus' Divine and Human Natures

It is a profound theological truth that Jesus had to be both fully human and fully divine in order to save us. In the last lesson we saw that Jesus our Savior had to be human so that His life and blood could pay the death penalty in our place. At the same time, He had to be divine in order to be the sinless, perfect sacrifice required by God.

This lesson shows that our brother and high priest Jesus had to be human so that He could understand our temptations and thus be a sympathetic representative for us before God. At the same time, He had to be divine in order to come into God's holy, perfect presence and intercede perfectly on our behalf. Theologian John Frame addresses Jesus' two natures:

> "The two natures of Christ do not make him a kind of divine-human hybrid. As the Council of Chalcedon stated, his two natures are 'unconfused and unchanged,' as well as 'undivided and unseparated.'
>
> "So even in the person of Christ, where divinity and humanity are most intimately related, the two are distinct... Jesus is fully God and fully man, not some kind of intermediate being."[17]

We need to grasp the truth of Jesus' full divinity and humanity and let it make a home in our hearts and minds, allowing it to encourage us in our faith.

Part II: Studying Scripture

Read Hebrews 2:10-13

1. Jesus' Suffering

a) In v. 10, it is God ("he" or "him") who perfected Jesus, the founder or leader of our salvation. The idea of Jesus being perfected does not imply anything lacking in Christ's character, but means completion or achievement of the highest goal. What goal was attained for believers through Jesus' suffering and death, according to v. 10?

b) In v. 11, it is Jesus ("he" or "the one") who sanctifies or makes people holy. Jesus and those He sanctifies have one origin (literally, "are all of one"), meaning either that they both have God as their Father, or they both have a human nature. What is the relationship between Jesus and those He sanctifies?

c) It is a common theme in the New Testament that the sufferings of Jesus and the salvation of humans are bound together. Why does the suffering of the sanctifier create a close bond with the one being sanctified or made holy?

2. Jesus' Brothers and Sisters

a) The people redeemed by Christ's suffering are referred to with family language. For example, find three words associated with family relationships in v. 10-13. (Note that the term brothers should be understood to mean brothers and sisters here.)

b) Jesus cares about the believers and is not ashamed to call them His brothers and sisters. What does it mean to you that Jesus sees you as a brother or sister, and how should you act in response? In what practical ways can we show that we are not ashamed of Jesus?

3. Jesus' Affinity with Believers

The first proof text regarding Jesus' humanity was covered in the previous lesson. Now we come to three more Old Testament proof texts that illustrate Jesus' affinity with humans.

a) Read Psalm 22:22, the second proof text. You may be familiar with the opening lament of this messianic psalm which Jesus quoted on the cross, "My God, my God, why have you forsaken me?" (Psalm 22:1). However, by the end of the psalm the psalmist turns his lament into joyful confidence in God's deliverance.

Looking at the quote in Hebrews 2:12, how did Jesus share His joy over God's deliverance, just as we should?

b) Read Isaiah 8:17, the third proof text. This is a messianic passage that speaks of the Messiah and God's people facing the danger of war. Looking at the quote in Hebrews 2:13a, how did Jesus respond to adversity, just like all believers should?

c) Read Isaiah 8:18, the fourth proof text and a continuation of the third one. It indicates that when the Messiah and God's chosen people trust God to save in the face of war, they are signs and symbols to the rest of the world regarding God's faithfulness. Thus Jesus and His church are evidence to others that God can be trusted to save even in the worst of times.

What would your acquaintances say about the way you exhibit trust in God during hard times? How will you learn to trust Him more?

d) The chart below summarizes the four proof texts in Hebrews 2. Which one of these aspects of Jesus' humanity is most meaningful to you and why?

Jesus' Humanity

Verse   Summary and Proof Text

2:6-8   Humans are meant to rule creation; Jesus rules now (Ps. 8:4-6).

2:12   Jesus identifies with believers, His true brothers and sisters (Ps. 22:22).

2:13a   Jesus puts His faith and trust in God, as all people should (Is. 8:17).

2:13b   Jesus and His people are signs of God's faithfulness (Is. 8:18).

Read Hebrews 2:14-18

4. Jesus' Incarnation

The Son was eternally divine before He became human. The Son, the second person of the Trinity, came to earth at His first coming and took on human form without ceasing to have a divine nature. He became God incarnate, meaning "God in the flesh," and He was Immanuel, meaning "God with us."

a) The Son of God had to become like the creatures He intended to save. He had to share their humanity by taking on flesh and blood so He could represent them and pay the death penalty for their sin. What does Jesus accomplish by His suffering and death according to the verses below?

2:14   He destroys: _____

2:15-16 He delivers: _____

2:17   He is merciful: _____

          He atones: _____

2:18   He helps: _____

b) In v. 16, Jesus helps (literally, "takes hold of") the offspring of Abraham, not angels. This could mean that Jesus helps humans rather than spirits such as angels. Another interpretation is that Jesus saves His church, the true descendants of Abraham (Galatians 3:7, 29), rather than immortal angels who do not need to be saved from death. What would it look like if our lives genuinely demonstrated the joy and assurance of being in Jesus' firm grasp, free from fear of God's condemnation?

c) To be tempted is not a sin, but giving in to temptation is. Think of one area of temptation you struggle with. What will you do to discover what God says about dealing with your particular area of temptation?

d) How will it help you deal with all kinds of temptation to know that Jesus overcame by obediently relying on God's word?

5. Jesus' Atoning Work

Jesus had to be human in order to make atonement or propitiation for our sins (v. 17). Propitiation means appeasing God's wrath by means of a suitable sacrifice so we can come before Him. Only the perfect and final sacrifice of Jesus' blood could appease God.

a) Many people's mistaken attitude regarding God's wrath is, "God's not so mad and I'm not so bad." Why do you suppose people have generally lost a sense of sin and a sense of fear with regard to God's wrath?

b) Sometimes people have to come to the end of their resources before they turn to God in humility and confess their sin. Think of a time when you finally came to the end of yourself. How did you discover that when Christ is all you have, Christ is all you need? How will your experience help you deal patiently with those who deny their need for Christ?

c)   Why is it futile for people to try to attain atonement (propitiation) for their sins by their own works?

d)   What wrong attitude do people convey about the sufficiency of Christ's atoning work when they try to add to it with their own works?

6.   Why Jesus Has to Be Human to Save Us

Scripture teaches us that belief in the humanity of Jesus Christ is essential for Christians. Take time to meditate on the following five reasons why the Son's humanity is necessary for our salvation. Which two are most important to you? Commit those to memory in order to encourage yourself and others.

1)   Only a human blood sacrifice could atone for our sins.
2)   Only a human could be our representative in covenant obedience.
3)   Only a human could fulfill the office of high priest.
4)   Only a human could mediate between humans and God.
5)   Only humans are to rule the world for God.

Part III: Personal Application and Growth

Today's lesson points to several important truths that apply to our personal lives. Allow these truths to penetrate your mind, soften your heart, deepen your faith and affect your behavior to help you continually grow in Christ.

1.   Jesus suffered temptation and will help us when we are tempted.

Jesus sympathizes, comforts and strengthens us so we can overcome temptation. Similarly, we are to sympathize with others in their weakness. Think of someone you know who is struggling with temptation in an area where you have struggled. What practical steps will you take this week to show compassion and offer hope?

2. Jesus is our sympathetic high priest when we fail to resist temptation.

Author John Piper says some things never change; the problem of a guilty conscience is as old as Adam and Eve. He reminds Christians that under the new covenant they are forgiven and no longer have to carry the burden of guilt for sin:

> "So here we are in the modern age – the age of science, Internet, organ transplants, instant messaging, cell phones – and our problem is fundamentally the same as always: Our conscience condemns us. We don't feel good enough to come to God...
>
> "We feel God's purity and perfection so keenly that everything about us seems unsuitable in his presence. But then we remember that Jesus is 'sympathetic.' He feels *with* us, not *against* us. This awareness of Christ's sympathy makes us bold to come. He knows our cry. He tasted our struggle. He bids us come with confidence when we feel our need."[18]

What past failure in your walk with God keeps coming to your mind? Perhaps it persists because you have not yet asked for or accepted the forgiveness obtained by your sympathetic high priest, Jesus Christ. Today express your repentance to God, ask His forgiveness, turn over any lingering guilt, anger, or disappointment, and accept His reassurance of forgiveness.

3. Believers are spiritual brothers and sisters to Jesus and to each other.

Starting now, try to develop the habit of greeting Christians as Brother or Sister, either verbally or silently in your mind. Why will this habit help conform your thinking and feelings to Christ's?

Part IV: Closing Devotion
by Charles Spurgeon

Oh, what a relationship there is between Christ and the believer! The believer can say, "I have a Brother in heaven; I may be poor, but I have a Brother who is rich, and is a King, and will He allow me to lack while He is on His throne? Oh, no! He loves me; He is my Brother."

Believer, wear this blessed thought like a golden ring on the finger of recollection, and use it as the King's own seal, stamping it on the petitions of your faith with confidence of success.

Christ became human that He might know our wants and sympathize with us. He "in every respect has been tempted as we are, yet without sin" (Hebrews 4:15). In all our sorrows we have His sympathy. Temptation, pain, disappointment, weakness, weariness, poverty – He knows them all, for He has felt all.

Remember this, Christian, and let it comfort you. However difficult and painful your road, it is marked by the footsteps of your Savior; and even when you reach the dark valley of the shadow of death, and the deep waters of the swelling Jordan, you will find His footprints there. In all places wherever we go, He has been our forerunner; each burden we have to carry has once been laid on the shoulders of Immanuel, God with us. Take courage![19]

SECTION II

THE WORK OF JESUS CHRIST

(WHAT HE HAS DONE)

❧ Lesson 5 ❧

The Greatest Prophet

Hebrews 3:1-6

Part I: Setting the Stage

Purpose

In the third chapter of Hebrews the author begins to focus on the work of Jesus Christ. Jesus perfectly fulfills Israel's earthly offices of prophet, priest and king. It is important for us to be familiar with these three offices because Jesus' fulfillment of each one is basic to our salvation. With regard to the office of prophet, Jesus is far superior to the esteemed prophet Moses.

Look for the following application points in this lesson:

1. Jesus perfectly fulfills the office of prophet by mediating God's plan of salvation.
2. There is only one people of God, the true church, made up of believers from all eras.
3. Those belonging to God's household remain faithful to Christ to the end.

Offices of Prophet, Priest and King

As we have already seen, the first two chapters of Hebrews dealt with the *person* of Jesus Christ. He is one person with two natures, divine and human. Jesus is the divine Son of God, superior to angels. He is the promised Messiah, our Savior, and our human brother.

Having established who Jesus Christ is, the author now turns to the *work* of Jesus Christ. Jesus' work perfectly fulfills the three offices of Israel: prophet, priest and king. These functions are also called the threefold office of Christ. Everything Jesus does as the Messiah falls into these three categories.

God ordained the leadership offices of prophet, priest and king in the Old Testament era as the means by which He related to His people and governed Israel. These offices became more distinct in Israel as time went on:

- Prophets spoke for God and revealed Him to the people.
- Priests represented the people to God and appealed to God for their salvation through sacrifice and prayer.
- Kings ruled in Israel as God's representative.

Fulfillment by the Messiah

The 16th century Reformer John Calvin is credited with being the first major theologian to describe Jesus Christ's work in terms of the threefold office of prophet, priest and king:

> "Therefore, that faith may find in Christ a solid ground of salvation, and so rest in Him, we must set out with this principle, that the office which He received from the Father consists of three parts. For He was appointed Prophet, King, and Priest..."[20]

Prophet: Jesus is the perfect prophet who conveyed the fullness of God's plan of salvation at His first coming, continues to proclaim it today through His body, the church, and will bring it to completion at the end times.

Priest: Jesus is the perfect high priest who obtained our salvation by His substitutionary sacrifice on the cross and His continual intercession on our behalf in God's presence. We are allowed to draw near to God only by faith in Christ's atoning work, not on the basis of our own works.

King: Jesus is the perfect king who was exalted for His obedience on the cross and rules the world at the right hand of God. He will come in glory at the end times to consummate God's kingdom. Believers will co-reign with Christ forever as heirs of salvation.

A Prophet's Role

The prophets of the Old Testament were chosen by God to speak on His behalf to the people and their leaders. True prophets (*naviim*, "called ones") proclaimed only what God told them and they were not free to refrain from proclaiming it. They called for such things as repentance, true worship, social justice, and covenant obedience.

In addition to forthtelling God's word, prophets were often engaged in foretelling the future. Their predictions sometimes took the form of unconditional prophecies of judgment that inevitably came to pass, or unconditional promises of God's glorious restoration through the Messiah after the punishment of exile.

At other times the prophets made conditional prophecies whose outcome depended on conditions such as people's repentance. For instance, Jonah prophesied that Nineveh would be destroyed, but God withheld judgment when the people repented (Jonah 3:4-10).

Moses was the first great prophet and the greatest prophet in the Old Testament. His role in God's revelatory and redemptive work prepared God's people for the ultimate revelation and redemption brought by the Messiah, Jesus Christ. We can be encouraged by the fact that Jesus is a prophet far superior to Moses.

Part II: Studying Scripture

Read Hebrews 3:1-2

The opening word "therefore" connects these verses to the previous discussion of unity between Jesus and His spiritual brothers and sisters.

1. A Heavenly Calling

a) In v. 1, how does the author address the readers? The word "holy" means set apart for God. Note that the idea of Christian brethren includes women as well as men.

b) What does the author say these believers have in common?

c) The Lord calls to us with encouragement *from* heaven, and calls us *to* heaven, our final destination. Give some practical examples of how the knowledge that you are headed for heaven shapes your decisions, such as how to spend your time and money.

d) Since our Christian brothers and sisters are sharers or partakers (literally, "partners") with us in this heavenly calling, how should a common destination of heaven impact the way you think about and interact with difficult Christians you meet in your local church?

2. Consider Jesus

a) In order to strengthen our faith we are to seriously consider (literally, "observe") Jesus. According to v. 1, which of Jesus' roles should we meditate on in particular?

b) Apostles ("ones sent forth") were the New Testament equivalent of Old Testament prophets ("ones called") in that both were chosen by God to declare His word, and both were ambassadors empowered with God's authority. Apostles were greater than prophets because the apostles saw the fulfillment of God's saving promises in Jesus Christ.

This is the only place in Scripture where Jesus is called an apostle. The author may have chosen the title apostle rather than prophet to maintain a distinction between the old and new eras of revelation. What did the author teach earlier to prepare us for the idea that God sent Jesus into the world to be an apostle or prophet (see Hebrews 1:1-2)?

c) Read Deuteronomy 18:15-18. What did Moses predict about Jesus almost 1,500 years before His birth?

d) Read John 5:45-47. What did Jesus say to confirm that He fulfilled Moses' prophecy?

3. Similar to Moses

a) In v. 2, what is one way Jesus is similar to the prophet Moses?

b) Read Numbers 12:6-8. Moses mediated the old covenant of law and was commended in Scripture as someone having a unique status with God. How does this passage indicate that Moses was no ordinary prophet?

c) Why is it appropriate for the author of Hebrews to compare Jesus with Moses?

Read Hebrews 3:3-6

4. Greater Than Moses

a) In v. 3a, what is one way Jesus is different from the prophet Moses?

b) In v. 3-4, what building term is identified with each of the following persons? Note that the word "house" can mean either a building structure or a household of people.

Moses: _____

Jesus: _____

God: _____

c) Looking at the above answers we see that the author considers Jesus to be on the same level with God, not Moses. How does this explain why Jesus has more glory than Moses, even though they were both faithful in their roles as mediators of God's covenants?

5. God's House

God's house is a figurative term for God's people, His household, the true church. There is only one house consisting of all believers in all eras. God is the builder of the house and Jesus is His divine agent.

God builds His house in two stages: first, the Old Testament era represented by the prophet Moses; and second, the New Testament era represented by Jesus. The contrast between the two eras is summarized in the chart below:

One Household Built in Two Stages

	Old Testament Era (v. 5)	New Testament Era (v. 6a)
Leader?	Moses the prophet	Jesus the apostle
His stature?	Servant in the house	Son over the house
His testimony?	Christ will come *(implied)*	Christ has come *(implied)*

---

a) Looking at the above chart, what is the difference in stature between Moses and Jesus?

b) In v. 5, the word describing Moses as a servant is not the usual Greek word *doulos* which indicates slavery or compulsory service. Rather, the word for servant is *therapon,* used only here in the New Testament. Moses was no ordinary servant. *Therapon* implies dignified and freely chosen service to someone superior, with a healing or therapeutic quality about such service. How does this explanation increase your appreciation of Moses as God's servant?

c) In v. 6a, although the servant has an honored position in God's house, why would a son be worthy of more glory than a servant?

d) Read Ephesians 2:19-22 and I Timothy 3:14-15. What kind of response does it bring out in you to realize that you belong to a growing, living household of faith that spans the ages?

6. Our Faithfulness

a) In v. 6b, how can we know if we are part of God's household, the true church?

b) Read Jeremiah 9:23-24. What three things should we not boast about? What does God want us to glory in and boast about?

c) Read I Corinthians 1:30-31 where Paul quotes Jeremiah 9:24. What are four things Christ has done that believers may boast about?

d) U. S. Senate Chaplain Barry Black, the first African-American to hold the position, speaks of persevering in faith despite obstacles. He sees God's hand in his life all the way from the hood to the Hill, from a Baltimore public housing project to Capitol Hill:

> "And right up front, I want to state that the critical factor in this happy ending was a sovereign Providence. God was working strongly in my life. But just as important, God wasn't someone I discovered for myself – I've had a lot of help.
>
> "Early in life, my mother, Pearline, convinced me that God had created me for something special... She took my siblings and me to church with her. She worked hard to give me a Christian education. She planted in my spirit a love for the sacred Scriptures. And God smiled on her efforts and blessed them...
>
> "God also opened and closed doors on my behalf, and used my own marital and parenting challenges to make me less selfish. He implanted in me a resolve to weather life's tragedies and setbacks, and He developed my ability

to see them as opportunities to climb higher on faith's ladder."[21]

Looking back over your faith journey, where do you most clearly see how God has worked strongly in your life to help you hold fast to your confidence and hope in Christ?

Part III: Personal Application and Growth

Today's lesson points to several important truths that apply to our personal lives. Allow these truths to penetrate your mind, soften your heart, deepen your faith and affect your behavior to help you continually grow in Christ.

1.   Jesus perfectly fulfills the office of prophet by mediating God's plan of salvation.

Countless believers prior to Jesus Christ had to be content merely with God's promise of salvation foretold by the prophets. How will you express your appreciation to God today for the privilege of living in the era of Christ's fulfillment of that promise?

2.   There is only one people of God, the true church, made up of believers from all eras.

The true church consists of all true believers in every period of history and every part of the world. This week find out the names of missionaries and church planters your church supports, whom Christ is using to build His household around the world. Put their prayer cards on your refrigerator or someplace visible to remind you to pray for them and send encouraging notes over the next twelve months.

3. Those belonging to God's household remain faithful to Christ to the end.

This week identify three specific challenges to your faith, whether they are in the form of temptations, persecution, apathy, hardship, doubts, or something else. What steps will you take to address these challenges so you may overcome them and remain faithful to Christ?

Part IV: Closing Devotion
by Charles Spurgeon

Believer, perseverance is the badge of true saints. The Christian life is not only a beginning in the ways of God, but also a continuance in the same as long as life lasts. They alone are true conquerors, and shall be crowned at the last, who continue till war's trumpet is blown no more.

Perseverance is, therefore, the target of all our spiritual enemies. The *world* does not object to your being a Christian for a time, but will tempt you to cease your pilgrimage. The *flesh* will seek to ensnare you and to prevent you from pressing on to glory.

Satan will make many a fierce attack on your perseverance; it will be the mark for all his arrows. He will strive to hinder you in service, make you weary of suffering, attack your steadfastness, and assail your doctrinal sentiments.

Therefore, wear your shield close upon your armor, Christian, and call out mightily unto God, that by His Spirit you may endure to the end.[22]

⮞ Lesson 6 ⮜

Revealing God's Saving Word

Hebrews 3:7-19

Part I: Setting the Stage

Purpose

We saw in the previous lesson that God is building one household of believers in two building stages: the Old Testament era represented by the prophet Moses, and the New Testament era represented by the greater prophet Jesus. It is important for us to remember that living in God's household in any era means taking part in corporate Christian life and obeying God's house rules. We are to respond to God's revealed word with believing and obedient hearts.

Look for the following application points in this lesson:

1. Christians belong to God's household and willingly obey His rules.
2. People should respond in belief to God's saving word.
3. Those that permanently reject Jesus Christ will never have salvation.

A Superb Illustration

Rather than quoting several proof texts to support his line of reasoning like he did in each of the first two chapters of Hebrews, the author presents just one proof text for the third and fourth chapters combined. He chooses a well-known passage from Psalm 95 to illustrate his point so completely that no other proof text is needed to show Jesus' superiority over Moses.

The readers of Hebrews would have been extremely familiar with Psalm 95 as a call to worship. The overall theme of the psalm is people's response to God's salvation. Believers rightfully respond with joyful praise and gratitude to God the Creator and Savior. Unbelievers like the ancient Israelites in the desert wrongfully respond with hardened hearts, rebellion, sin, and disobedience.

The psalm's application would have been clear to the readers of Hebrews. They all knew that the Israelites in the wilderness faced a permanent penalty for rebelling against the great prophet Moses, rejecting the salvation he accomplished in the Exodus, and disobeying the covenant of law he mediated.

How much more, then, will people be punished for rejecting Jesus the Son, one far greater than Moses, and for rejecting both the perfect salvation he obtained on the cross and the new covenant of salvation He mediated!

The Rebellion
The Israelites' rebellion lasted throughout forty years of wilderness wandering. It was all the more egregious because it followed God's greatest saving act of the Old Testament, the Exodus from slavery in Egypt.

Soon after leaving Egypt the Israelites complained about the lack of food and water, charging Moses with treason and threatening to execute him. It was ultimately God whom they put on trial. God the Rock was guiltless but bore the unfair judgment as Moses struck Him with a rod. Moses named the area Meribah ("quarreling") and Massah ("testing") as a witness to Israel's accusations and lack of faith (Exodus 17:1-7).

The Israelites' rebellious attitude continued when they refused to enter the Promised Land of Canaan at the first opportunity God provided. They feared the powerful residents of Canaan and did not trust God to keep His saving word. As a result, God vowed never to let the adults of that generation enter Canaan except for Caleb and Joshua, the two Israelite spies who had encouraged the people to obey God (Numbers 14:22-23, 38).

Although God provided miraculous manna, quail and water in the wilderness, the people's accusations and grumbling continued. Toward the end of the forty years their ongoing rebellion caused Moses to name another place Meribah (Numbers 20:1-13).

Lest We Forget

It would be wise for Christians today to become well acquainted with the episode of the Israelites' rebellion, because Biblical writers frequently refer to it as the quintessential illustration of the consequences of disobedience to God's word. We should also make an effort to pass the story on to future generations for their benefit.

The historical account of the Israelites' rebellion is so compelling that listeners cannot help but find themselves back in time, caught up in the drama. We would be no different than the rebellious Israelites if it were not for God's grace. What an encouragement that God has given us the gift of faith in Jesus Christ so that we might live joyfully as part of His household.

Part II: Studying Scripture

Those who belong to God's household respond to His voice with glad hearts. His house rules are for our benefit and we are to obey willingly. Unbelievers, on the other hand, harden their hearts when they hear God's word and refuse to be part of God's household.

1. Household Rules

a) Before we read this lesson's Scripture passages, let us take a moment to think about family life. When you were growing up, what was one of the rules in your home? Did you find it easy or difficult to comply with the rule? Why?

b) Parents establish rules in the home to accomplish a variety of good purposes. Give examples of reasonable household rules that could help a family meet the following goals:

Keep order: _____

Ensure safety: _____

Develop character: _____

Build relationships: _____

c) Rules should be a means to relationship, not the substance of relationship. The happiest homes are where rules define what it looks like to live in a loving, caring relationship with others. Family members ultimately obey the rules out of love for each other, not due to legalism or fear of punishment. What is destructive about merely following the letter of the law rather than the spirit of the law?

d) Perhaps you have heard the axiom, "Rules without relationship lead to rebellion." Why do children rebel? How does a loving relationship between parents and children diminish a child's need for destructive rebellion? How can healthy independence be planned and gradually worked out?

e) Philanthropist Truett Cathy, founder of Chick-fil-A, has established several foster homes. He advises that a rocking chair is good medicine for a young child who needs discipline and loving.[23] A parent may sooth a troubled child by holding the child and rocking together. What other methods build harmonious relationships while upholding respect for house rules?

Read Psalm 95:1-7c

Believers have a heart of flesh, figuratively speaking, that is tender toward God and His household. The first half of Psalm 95 describes how a believer responds to God's salvation.

2. A Heart of Flesh

a) In v. 1, a poetic couplet describes a believer's response to the LORD's salvation in two similar ways. Write down the two halves of the couplet and notice how they correspond to each other (translations will vary). What does each half add to your understanding of the other?

First half: _____

Second half: _____

b) In v. 2, what attitudes do true believers have toward God? Which of these attitudes would you like to develop more fully in your worship of God?

c) In v. 3 and 6, find four titles for God. Why are all of these titles appropriate to use in our worship?

d) In v. 4-5, two related poetic couplets emphasize the fact that the whole earth belongs to God because He made it. Notice how the phrases correspond to each other (translations will vary):

> *"The depths of the earth"* relates to *"the sea."*
> *"The heights of the mountains"* relates to *"the dry land."*

How does the mention of God's hand at the beginning and end of v. 4-5 affirm His ownership and control of the earth? This is anthropomorphic language, attributing human characteristics to God for literary effect.

e) In v. 6, how should believers respond to God the Creator? Note that the Hebrew word for "worship" means to prostrate oneself. What attitude do we convey when we get physically low before God? Would those closest to you say this is your attitude toward God? Why or why not?

f) In v. 7, what phrase relates to "people of His pasture" (translations will vary)? What do these images tell us about our relationship with God?

Read Psalm 95:7d-11

The second half of Psalm 95 is a sharp contrast to the first half. In the second half, unbelievers respond to God's salvation with a disobedient heart of stone.

No one, especially those who belong to God's household, should harden their hearts in response to hearing God's voice. Disobedience is disastrous whether today or 3,500 years ago when the Israelites rebelled in the wilderness.

3. A Heart of Stone

a) In v. 7d, the places Meribah ("quarreling") and Massah ("testing") represent the Israelites' continual rebellion against God during their wilderness wandering. The more their hearts strayed and hardened, the more they demanded that God prove Himself. For those with hearts of stone, why is God's provision never enough proof of His love?

b) In v. 9, why was there no excuse for the Israelites' lack of faith? Give some examples.

c) The Exodus was the greatest display of God's salvation in the Old Testament, but when God brought the Israelites to the Promised Land of Canaan, they initially refused to enter due to lack of faith in His promises. In v. 11, how did God respond to their unbelief?

Read Hebrews 3:7-11

The author of Hebrews quotes the second half of Psalm 95 as a proof text to remind his readers of the danger of failing to believe God's saving word.

4. Relevance Today

a) In v. 7, who is the real speaker of Psalm 95 according to the author of Hebrews?

b) The word "Today" and the use of the present tense make the Holy Spirit's warning against unbelief applicable in any time period. For example:

- In Moses' time during the wilderness wandering (around 1500 B.C.)
- In David's time when Psalm 95 was written (around 1000 B.C.)
- In the 1st century when Hebrews was written
- In the 21st century during our lives

How would you use this passage to answer those who say the Old Testament is irrelevant for us in the 21st century?

c) In v. 8, the author refers to rebellion and testing or trials in general terms rather than mentioning the wilderness locations of Meribah and Massah from Psalm 95. How does the author's generalized reference make it easier for us to apply the Spirit's warning to our lives today?

d) In v. 11, God does not react to unbelief with indifference. It provokes His wrath and yields eternal consequences. What does God swear will inevitably happen to unbelievers? Note that God's rest symbolizes salvation.

Read Hebrews 3:12-19

5. Turning Hearts Toward Home

a) The author knows that *professing* faith is not the same thing as *possessing* faith. In v. 12, although all the readers have made a confession of faith in Christ, what will eventually happen to those in their midst who do not truly believe?

b) Apostasy (falling away or turning away) is the deliberate, permanent rejection of God. Unbelievers inevitably fall away from God in the end. True Christians, on the other hand, will never fall away.

If Christians want assurance of faith they should act like believers, not like unbelievers with a hard heart. Believers should turn their hearts toward home, toward God's house. In v. 13, how can believers help each other?

c) In v. 14, how can Christians have assurance they are true believers?

6. Responding to Salvation

a) Although we cannot look at others and know who is saved, a person's refusal to live by God's word over the years is a sign of an unbelieving heart. What word in each verse below describes an unbeliever's response to God?

3:16 _____

3:17 _____

3:18 _____

b) Why is constant gratitude for God's salvation a powerful restraint against developing a heart of stone?

Part III: Personal Application and Growth

Today's lesson points to several important truths that apply to our personal lives. Allow these truths to penetrate your mind, soften your heart, deepen your faith and affect your behavior to help you continually grow in Christ.

1. Christians belong to God's household and willingly obey His rules.

What steps will you take this week to follow God's household rules with the proper heart motivation? How will your improved attitude promote loving relationships with others?

2. People should respond in belief to God's saving word.

Start today to keep a daily gratitude journal for a month. Write down the ways God showers His saving blessings on you each day. Meditate on how your faith in God's saving promises grows stronger the more you acknowledge Him.

3. Those that permanently reject Jesus Christ will never have salvation.

Pray for someone in your life who claims to be an agnostic or atheist, someone who rejects salvation in Christ. Which day this week will you invite him or her to have coffee together so you might gently share your belief in God and Christ? You may end up feeling your offer has no effect, but perhaps God will use you as His instrument to reach this person.

Part IV: Closing Devotion
by Charles Spurgeon

Believer, a heart of flesh is known by its *tenderness concerning sin.* To indulge a foul imagination or allow a wild desire to tarry even for a moment is quite enough to make a heart of flesh grieve before the Lord. The heart of stone calls a great iniquity nothing, but not so the heart of flesh.

The heart of flesh is *tender of God's will* and quivers like an aspen leaf in every breath of heaven. The natural will is cold, hard iron, which is not to be hammered into form.

In the fleshy heart there is a *tenderness of affections.* The hard heart does not love the Redeemer, but the renewed heart burns with affection towards Him. The hard heart is selfish and coldly demands, "Why should I weep for sin? Why should I love the Lord?" But the heart of flesh says, "Lord, You know that I love You; help me to love You more!"

A tender heart is the best defense against sin and the best preparation for heaven. Have you this heart of flesh?[24]

❧ Lesson 7 ❦

Revealing God's Eternal Rest

Hebrews 4:1-13

Part I: Setting the Stage

Purpose

Believers are on a faith journey. We are travelers longing for home, yearning to be at rest with God. The prophet Moses led God's people to the physical Promised Land of Canaan, a symbol of God's rest, yet it was an incomplete rest. Only the perfect prophet Jesus reveals and brings us all the way home to God's spiritual, eternal, divine rest. It is important for us to comprehend the truth that we enter God's rest now and forever by faith in Jesus Christ.

Look for the following application points in this lesson:

1. Entering God's rest means enjoying fellowship with God due to Christ's atonement.
2. Believers enter God's rest now and forever by faith in Jesus Christ.
3. We must put our faith in Christ while there is still time.

What Is God's Rest?

A discussion of God's rest involves multiple aspects. Three key concepts associated with God's rest are location, relationship, and completion.

Location

God's rest is often represented in the Old Testament by the physical Promised Land of Canaan. Life in Canaan was intended to be physically settled and safe from the dangers of war and wilderness wandering, a life marked by peace, work, and prosperity. God's people were to live in fellowship with Him. To enter Canaan the Israelites had to have faith in God demonstrated by obedience to His word. Covenant obedience was the basis for remaining in the land.

Canaan was also a symbol of heaven, the ultimate destination for God's people. The patriarchs looked beyond the land of Canaan to the invisible, lasting reality of heaven. They knew they were sojourners on earth seeking a heavenly homeland prepared by God. All believers are headed for heaven, the place where Jesus now bodily lives.

Relationship

The expression "to enter God's rest" also means to live in the spiritual presence of God, at peace with God because of Christ's saving work. It means salvation and fellowship with God. To enter God's rest is to enjoy a loving covenant relationship with God through salvation in Christ. Believers enter God's rest now and forever by faith in Christ during this lifetime.

Completion

God entered His rest after His work of Creation was finished. Similarly, believers enter God's eternal rest when life is finished. God's eternal rest is not an idle or passive existence, for God actively reigns and upholds Creation. Believers in heaven will actively worship God, co-reign with Christ, feast, and enjoy fellowship with the saints.

Entering God's Rest

The author of Hebrews focuses on how to enter God's spiritual rest. He talks about entering God's rest (*katapausis*) in this lifetime by faith in Jesus Christ, which enables us to enter God's divine, eternal sabbath-rest (*sabbatismos*) upon death.

Interestingly, the author does not mention the weekly Sabbath observance (*sabbaton*) which reminds people to behave as those who have entered God's rest.[25] The emphasis in Hebrews is instead on entering God's rest in the first place.

Unbelievers Will Never Enter

In the last lesson we saw that the Israelites rebelled against God shortly after leaving Egypt in the Exodus. Their disobedience is the subject of Psalm 95, the author's current proof text. God swore an oath in His wrath that the disobedient Israelites would never enter His rest. God's oath, recorded by David in Psalm 95:11, is based on Moses' account of the wilderness rebellion in Deuteronomy 1:34-35. The broader implication of God's oath is that no unbeliever in any age will ever enter His rest.

God's oath or vow means that the thing He swears will inevitably occur. It will not depend on conditions that could change the outcome of what is promised. God makes only a few oaths in Scripture, three of which are integral to the book of Hebrews. As our study progresses we will see that these three vows together prove the certainty of God's saving word, giving us assurance of salvation and encouragement to keep the faith.

Part II: Studying Scripture

Read Hebrews 4:1-8

God's offer for believers to enter His rest is still valid in our day, "Today." The Holy Spirit promises all who have faith in Jesus Christ that they will enter God's rest. We should remember, however, that there will come a time when the offer is no longer valid. Upon death or Christ's return it will be too late for those who have failed to put their faith in Jesus Christ. People must accept God's offer while there is time.

1. God's Offer

a) In v. 1, what phrase implies that God's offer may not always be available in the future?

b) Possibly not all the readers who professed faith in Christ would turn out to be true believers. True believers should not feel superior to unbelievers in this regard, though, for they are saved by grace alone, not by their own efforts. Why do you think the author says believers should "fear" for anyone in their midst who does not seem to have faith in Christ?

c) In v. 2, the good news of salvation came to the ancient Israelites by way of their godly spies, Joshua and Caleb, who trusted that God's plan for entering Canaan would be successful. Why did the Israelites fail to benefit from the good news?

d) In v. 3a, how do we accept God's offer to enter His rest in this lifetime?

e) Read Deuteronomy 6:10-12 and 12:10. List some of the material blessings associated with life in Canaan that the disobedient Israelites forfeited due to disbelief in God's word:

Deut. 6:10 _____

Deut. 6:11 _____

Deut. 12:10 _____

f) Why do unbelievers in our age or any age fail to benefit from the good news of God's salvation?

2. God's Oath

a) The author has already said God swore in His wrath that the unbelieving Israelites would never enter His rest (3:11). Now this oath of judgment is repeated two more times (4:3, 5). When something significant is stated three times in close proximity in Scripture, the repetition is similar to underlining or bold-face print. It is meant to get our attention. What effect does it have on you to read this oath of judgment three times?

b) Considering what God accomplished for His people in the Exodus from Egypt, why do you suppose the Israelites' rebellion grieved and angered God so deeply?

c) God's oath against the unbelieving Israelites extends to all people who reject His plan of salvation. Whether He reveals salvation in the Exodus or ultimately through the cross, God's ancient oath is just as relevant today as ever: unbelievers will never enter His rest, His presence. How will His oath motivate you to share the gospel with an unbelieving friend?

3. Results of Rejecting the Offer

a) The rebellion of the Israelites constituted deliberate and permanent rejection of God. In return, God let them perish in their sin so that none of the rebellious Israelites entered Canaan. It has been estimated that nearly ninety adults must have died each day on average during forty years of wilderness wandering. What impact does it have on you to know that God kept His oath of judgment?

b) God's punishment for persistent, sinful unbelief is the same today as it was for the Israelites 3,500 years ago: unbelievers will never enter God's rest. Scripture does not support a universalistic view of salvation in which everyone is saved. In v. 6, how is it confirmed that some people will not be saved?

c) People at times worry that after death unbelievers will be standing at the locked gates of heaven begging God to let them in. That is not the picture we get from Scripture. Heaven is open wide to all who put their faith in Christ, but unbelievers run the other way in rebellion. In your view, why would some people rather go to hell than trust in Christ?

4. Entering God's Rest Now

a) God's rest has been available to believers long before Abraham, Moses, or the Israelites. According to v. 3-4, when did God's rest begin?

b) In v. 7, the phrase "Today, if you hear His voice" means that God graciously offers His rest to each new generation. What warning accompanies God's offer?

c) Why do you suppose the author quotes God's offer and warning together three times in close proximity (3:7-8; 3:15; 4:7)?

d) In v. 8, if entering Canaan had actually fulfilled God's promise of rest, there would be no need for God to invite people living there centuries later to enter His rest. The fact that God's offer of rest was extended in

David's time in Psalm 95 and again in Hebrews indicates that Canaan symbolized a greater spiritual reality. How does it make you feel to know that God invites us in the 21ˢᵗ century to enter His rest, joining countless saints (believers) from throughout the ages?

e) Perhaps you have had a yearning to "go home" even when you are at home. This feeling reflects the truth that we are sojourners in this world seeking rest with God. Saint Augustine understood our longing when he wrote his famous prayer around A.D. 400,

> "You have made us for Yourself, and our heart is restless until it rests in You."[26]

Give a few examples of the kinds of things people rely on besides God to make their restless heart content. Why don't those things satisfy in the long run?

Read Hebrews 4:9-13

5. Entering God's 'Sabbath-Rest' Forever

In v. 9, the author uses a word for God's eternal sabbath-rest (*sabbatismos*) that is not found anywhere else in the Bible. Its meaning is not quite the same as the word for rest (*katapausis*) used in the other verses. *Sabbatismos* is God's own rest and involves continual resting from a finished activity. God eternally rests after His finished work of Creation.

a) In v. 9-10, believers are invited to participate in God's eternal sabbath-rest. They enter God's eternal rest at death when they cease from their labors, just as God ceased from His work of Creation. Describe some of the labors or sufferings you are looking forward to being done with at the end of life.

b) The only way to enter God's eternal sabbath-rest at death is to enter His rest by faith in Christ during life and then persevere in faith to the end. We need to be purposeful about persevering in faith. In v. 11a, what should be our attitude?

c) In v. 11a, the original Greek says "hasten" or "be eager." What does it look like to persevere in faith with eagerness? Describe what aspects of life after death you look forward to eagerly.

d) It will be too late for people to put faith in Christ if they wait until they have died. Why do you think so many people take the risk of putting off thinking about Christ and their eternal destiny?

6. Our Hearts Revealed

Hearing God's word always calls for a response, and people's responses are never neutral. People who believe God's word are assured they will enter His rest and enjoy His fellowship forever. On the other hand, people who react to God's word by hardening their hearts in unbelief will eventually fall away in disobedience to face eternal judgment.

a) In v. 12, God's word is compared to a sword, the sharpest weapon in an ancient arsenal. Considering the image figuratively, this is the perfect tool for God to probe the deepest recesses of our inner being. God's word penetrates and reveals the thoughts hidden in our heart, whether belief or unbelief.

    Give an example of a time when Scripture penetrated your own heart and revealed to you what was there. How did you feel and how did your life change as a result?

b) Taking v. 12-13 in a symbolic sense, explain in your own words why people are foolish to think they can enjoy the benefits of God's rest, His presence, while trying to hide their unbelief from Him.

c) Read Psalm 139:1-12. How does the psalmist confirm what the author of Hebrews is saying? How will you become more honest and open with God?

Part III: Personal Application and Growth

Today's lesson points to several important truths that apply to our personal lives. Allow these truths to penetrate your mind, soften your heart, deepen your faith and affect your behavior to help you continually grow in Christ.

1. Entering God's rest means enjoying fellowship with God due to Christ's atonement.

Because Christ has restored our broken relationship with God, what will you do starting today to draw closer to God, know Him better, and enjoy Him more?

2. Believers enter God's rest now and forever by faith in Jesus Christ.

We are to live every moment of every day with a reverent awareness of having entered God's rest, meaning we live in God's presence. The Reformer John Calvin's motto was *coram Deo* (Latin for "in the presence of God"). Create your own motto in any language to sum up an aspect of entering God's rest that is important to you (fellowship with God, peace, activity, eternity, etc.). How will your motto remind you to live as someone who has already entered God's rest?

3. We must put our faith in Christ while there is still time.

John Quincy Adams, sixth president of the United States, wrote a letter to his father stating that his hopes of a future life were founded upon the gospel of Jesus Christ.[27] Many years later on his deathbed Adams confirmed his faith, reassuring those present that he was content to leave his earthly life.

What letter, journal entry, or other evidence affirming your faith in Christ will you write this week, saving a copy among your important papers? How might it one day comfort and inspire your loved ones?

Part IV: Closing Devotion
by Charles Spurgeon

Believer, our hope in Christ for the future is the mainspring and the mainstay of our joy here. It will animate our hearts to think often of heaven, for all that we can desire is promised there. Here we are weary and toilworn, but yonder is the land of rest where the sweat of labor shall no more dampen the worker's brow, and fatigue shall be forever banished.

To those who are weary and spent, the word "rest" is full of heaven. We are always in the field of battle; we are so tempted within, and so mistreated by foes without, that we have little or no peace; but in heaven we shall enjoy the victory.

Nevertheless, let it never be said of us that we are dreaming about the *future* and forgetting the *present*; let the future sanctify the present to highest uses. Through the Spirit of God the hope of heaven is the most potent force for the product of virtue; it is a fountain of joyous effort, it is the corner stone of cheerful holiness. The man who has this hope in him goes about his work with vigor, for the joy of the Lord is his.[28]

❧ Lesson 8 ❧

The Greatest Priest

Hebrews 4:14-5:10

Part I: Setting the Stage

Purpose

This lesson brings us to the heart of the author's message. We can be encouraged in our faith because we have an ally in Jesus Christ who serves as our high priest. He is superior to the great high priest Aaron. It is important for us to realize that Christ's atoning work on the cross is made effective by His continual intercession for us in heaven as our high priest.

Look for the following application points in this lesson:

1. Jesus perfectly fulfills the office of high priest by His sacrifice and intercession.
2. Believers pray to God through Jesus Christ, their eternal high priest.
3. We should join in Christ's work of intercession by praying for others.

A Unique Book

The book of Hebrews is a gracious gift from above. It is the only place we learn about the high priestly ministry of Jesus Christ in heaven. As high priest He offered the final and complete sacrifice to cover our sin. He leads us into God's presence and He continually prays for us.

Theologian Louis Berkhof says Christ is praying that our faith may not cease and we may come out victorious in the end:

"It is a consoling thought that Christ is praying for us, even when we are negligent in our prayer life; that He is presenting to the Father those spiritual needs which were not present to our minds and which we often neglect to include in our prayers; and that He prays for our protection against the dangers of which we are not even conscious… The intercessory prayer of Christ is a prayer that never fails."[29]

A Bold Book

As the author presents the case for Christ's fulfillment of the offices of prophet, priest and king, he points out that the old Levitical priesthood and law are no longer needed. This is a radical departure from Jewish orthodoxy. It potentially exposed the author to the same accusations of heresy and treason punishable by death that had already led to the martyrdom of Stephen.

The author carefully backs up his arguments with Old Testament proof texts that defuse accusations that he might be promoting ideas of his own making. He points out clues in Scripture foretelling that the Levitical priesthood was temporary and one day would be fulfilled and replaced by the Messiah. Christ's work was both something new and a continuation of God's overall plan of salvation.

Worshiping God His Way

God is the one who determines how He is to be worshiped. In His gracious providence God has ordained that sinful people may approach Him by means of a representative *high priest* of His choosing, who appears in the *sanctuary* of His choosing, on the basis of a blood *sacrifice* of His choosing. The Levitical priesthood partially and temporarily satisfied those requirements until the time was right for Jesus Christ to bring complete and permanent fulfillment.

God established the Levitical priesthood through the Law of Moses. The Law provided a way for humans to pay the death penalty for sin by substituting an animal's blood. A priest symbolically transferred the worshiper's guilt to the animal, slaughtered it, and offered it to God as atonement for sin to obtain forgiveness. This partial atonement had to be repeated often.

Jesus' fulfillment of the Levitical system meant that God's people no longer needed an earthly priesthood to meet God's requirements for worshiping Him. God's requirements were fulfilled forever in Jesus Christ.

The book of Hebrews explains this fulfillment in some depth. Jesus has provided the perfect and final *sacrifice* and serves in the perfect *sanctuary* in heaven. He is our representative *high priest* who has opened the way into the heavenly holy places so we may follow Him into God's presence without fear of condemnation. We can draw near to God without an earthly priest because Jesus is our perfect, heavenly high priest. What a great encouragement to our faith.

Part II: Studying Scripture

Under Mosaic Law, the tribe of Levi was set apart for religious work. Out of the Levites the line of Aaron was designated for the priesthood. Aaron, Moses' brother, was the first and greatest Levitical high priest, and Aaron's four sons served as the first priests.

1. The Levitical or Aaronic Priesthood

a) Read Exodus 28:1-4. Why were the high priestly garments made of such costly materials?

b) How did the following items symbolize the fact that the high priest represented the people of Israel when he entered God's presence?

Ephod (see Exodus 28:9-12) _____

Breastpiece (see Exodus 28:21, 28-29) _____

_____

c) Read Numbers 16:3-5 and 17:1-8. Two large factions from the tribes of Levi and Reuben jealously challenged Aaron's appointment as high priest. What was the definitive proof that God had chosen Aaron's line for the priesthood?

Read Hebrews 4:14-16

2. Jesus, Our Unique High Priest

a) In v. 14, which phrases indicate Jesus' divinity? Why does Jesus' divine status ensure that God will listen to His pleas?

b) In v. 15, what indicates Jesus' humanity? Why does Jesus' human nature ensure that He can sympathize with us and therefore represent us whole-heartedly?

c) Jesus Christ's high priesthood is the reason we can draw near to God with confidence. In v. 16b, which word indicates what believers will receive at God's throne of grace because of Christ, instead of the punishment they deserve for yielding to temptation?

d) Again in v. 16b, which word indicates what believers will find in time of need, so they have the strength to resist temptation? How will you develop the habit of seeking this divine help in all kinds of situations?

Read Hebrews 5:1-10

3. The Order of Aaron

a) In v. 1, what was the purpose of the role of high priest?

b) In v. 2-3, why should the high priest show compassion to sinful people? How was the high priest supposed to deal with his own unintentional sin?

c) In v. 4, how did Aaron become high priest?

d) Read I Samuel 3:12-14. The Aaronic priesthood was limited and flawed. For example, the high priest Eli raised sons who used their priestly role to engage in extortion, greed, prostitution, and blasphemy. These types of intentional sins could not be atoned for by any sacrifices under Mosaic Law. What did God say would happen to Eli's family as a result?

4. The Order of Melchizedek

Jesus is a high priest in the order of Melchizedek, not the order of Aaron. We will study Melchizedek in more detail later in Lesson 11. For now it is enough to know he was a king and priest back in the time of Abraham, two thousand years before Christ. There were no other priests in the order of Melchizedek except the high priest Jesus Christ.

a) In v. 5, what is one thing Jesus had in common with high priests in the order of Aaron?

b) Yet why was Jesus not considered a high priest in the order of Aaron (see Hebrews 7:14)?

c) The author cites proof texts from two messianic psalms already mentioned in the first chapter (Psalms 2 and 110). In v. 5-6, what are two crucial aspects of Jesus' divinity that make His priesthood in the order of Melchizedek superior to the Aaronic or Levitical priesthood?

5. Learning Obedience Through Suffering

As discussed in Lesson 4, Jesus faced temptation in the wilderness at the start of His earthly ministry. Now the author refers to the end of Jesus' earthly ministry when Jesus was tempted to avoid the cross. Jesus prayed about His temptation in the Garden of Gethsemane after the Last Supper.

a) Read Luke 22:44. What does Luke's gospel teach us about the extent of Jesus' suffering and temptation as He prayed?

b) In Hebrews 5:7, what else do we learn about Jesus' suffering that shows He understands fear? These details are recorded only in Hebrews, not in the gospels. How does it comfort you to know Jesus understands and sympathizes when you cry out in anguish?

c) In v. 8, through His suffering at the Garden of Gethsemane and at His trial and crucifixion, Jesus "learned" obedience in that He actually experienced the obedience He was willing from eternity to do.

Think of a time you were willing in theory to do something difficult, such as make a personal sacrifice to care for a child or elderly parent, but then actually had to do it. What lessons did you learn from your obedience?

d) When Scripture says Jesus was "made perfect," this does not imply that Jesus was ever morally imperfect. Rather, the meaning is that He achieved or completed the highest goal. In v. 9, what did Jesus achieve by His suffering and obedience?

6.   Offering Intercessory Prayer

Jesus opened the heavenly holy places so that all believers may follow Him and enter. Theologian Hywel Jones pictures Jesus' intercession:

> "Just as Moses, and Joshua after him, were to lead the children of Israel out of Egypt, through the wilderness, and to the Promised Land, and Aaron and his descendants were to intercede for them on their way, so Jesus leads his people out of the kingdom of darkness, through this wilderness of a world, praying for them on their way to their heavenly home."[30]

a) Look up the definition of "intercede" in a dictionary and write it down. In your own words, what do you think is the main purpose of intercessory prayer?

b) Read John 17:13-21. This is part of what is called Jesus' high priestly prayer in the Garden of Gethsemane before His betrayal and arrest. It gives us an idea of how Jesus prays for believers. What touches your heart about the things Jesus asks God for on your behalf?

c) Author Oswald Chambers encourages us to imitate Christ in the priestly work of intercession:

> "The real business of your life as a saved soul is intercessory prayer. Wherever God puts you in circumstances, pray immediately, pray that His Atonement may be realized in other lives as it has been in yours. Pray for your friends *now;* pray for those with whom you come in contact *now...*
>
> "We see where other folks are failing, and we turn our discernment into the gibe of criticism instead of into intercession on their behalf...One of the subtlest burdens God ever puts on us as saints is this burden of discernment concerning other souls. He reveals things in order that we may take the burden of these souls before Him and form the mind of Christ about them."[31]

With this in mind, how will you improve your efforts at intercessory prayer for others?

d) Intercession does not mean we pray for people to succeed in everything they do. For instance, we do not pray that our enemies will be allowed to harm us or continue in wickedness, but that they will turn to the Lord and live in accordance with His word. Why is intercessory prayer a way of loving our enemies?

Part III: Personal Application and Growth

Today's lesson points to several important truths that apply to our personal lives. Allow these truths to penetrate your mind, soften your heart, deepen your faith and affect your behavior to help you continually grow in Christ.

1. Jesus perfectly fulfills the office of high priest by His sacrifice and intercession.

Theologian John Murray reminds us that Jesus' one-time sacrifice is tied up with His abiding priestly function:

> "He is a priest now, not to offer sacrifice but as the permanent personal embodiment of all the efficacy and virtue that accrued from the sacrifice once offered. And it is as such he ever continues to make intercession for his people. His ever-continuing and always-prevailing intercession is bound to the sacrifice once offered."[32]

In what practical ways will you approach life with renewed humility and confidence, knowing that Jesus continually intercedes for you before God on the basis of His shed blood?

2. Believers pray to God through Jesus Christ, their eternal high priest.

Because of Christ we do not need the intercession of an earthly priest in order for our prayers to be heard by God. We lift our prayers directly to God through His Son, Jesus Christ, our eternal high priest in heaven, praying as He would. Starting today, what phrase will you incorporate in your prayers to reflect your desire to pray to God the Father in the name of Jesus Christ?

3. We should join in Christ's work of intercession by praying for others.

This week when you find yourself criticizing other people's failings, what will you do to stop being critical and develop the habit of interceding for them in prayer, seeing them as Christ does?

Part IV: Closing Devotion
by Charles Spurgeon

Believer, how encouraging is the thought of the Redeemer's never-ceasing intercession for us. When we pray, He pleads for us; and when we are *not* praying, He is advocating our cause, and by His supplications shielding us from unseen dangers.

We little know what we owe to our Savior's prayers. When we reach the hilltops of heaven, and look back upon all the ways whereby the Lord our God has led us, how we shall praise Him who, before the eternal throne, undid the mischief which Satan was doing upon earth. How we shall thank Him because He never held His peace, but day and night pointed to the wounds upon His hands, and carried our names upon His breastplate!

O Jesus, what a comfort it is that You have pleaded our cause against our unseen enemies, counter-mined their mines, and unmasked their ambushes. Here is a matter for joy, gratitude, hope, and confidence.[33]

❧ Lesson 9 ❧

Attention! Seek Mature Teaching

Hebrews 5:11-6:12

Part I: Setting the Stage

Purpose
This lesson warns us to be ready for the author's upcoming teaching on Jesus and the royal priesthood of Melchizedek. It is important to recognize that such mature teaching will help our weak faith grow strong. We should not be content to drift aimlessly in immature faith, but strive for spiritual maturity.

Look for the following application points in this lesson:

1. Believers can strengthen their faith by studying mature Christian teaching.
2. An ongoing desire to seek mature teaching gives us assurance of salvation.
3. Rituals and church doctrine are essential companions to our faith life.

No More Drifting
The author interrupts himself to urge his readers to pay attention. It is time to press on toward spiritual maturity by studying mature teachings. Spiritually mature believers are better able to discern good from evil, withstand persecution, and pass on the faith. They also have assurance of salvation, for an ongoing desire to grow spiritually is in itself evidence of saving faith.

Keep in mind that the author of Hebrews makes a distinction between the terms "drift away" and "fall away." Drifting away, sometimes thought of as backsliding, is a careless, lazy attitude that results in immature faith. True believers who drift or backslide will not lose their salvation but will fail to enjoy the benefits of mature faith.

On the other hand, falling away is an intentional movement away from God toward apostasy. Apostasy is the deliberate, informed, permanent rejection of God. Those who fall away into apostasy are unbelievers who never had saving faith in the first place.

A Mixed Group

No one can look at people and know who is truly saved. Local churches are nearly always made up of a mix of believers and unbelievers, even if everyone makes a profession of faith. The author is aware he is addressing people in various spiritual states, including the following:

- True believers who are drifting in immaturity. They might drift indefinitely and their weak faith will make it hard to endure persecution and suffering. They will not lose their salvation but if they do not seek maturity they may suffer undue anxiety about whether they are saved. This seems to be the situation for most of the recipients of the letter.

- True believers who have confident faith. They seek mature teaching, imitate faithful believers, distance themselves from the obsolete Levitical worship system, and refuse to act like unbelievers who eventually fall away.

- Unbelievers who will never be regenerated by God. They will eventually lose interest in the things of God, their hearts will harden, and they will fall away into apostasy.

Press On To Maturity

The philosopher Blaise Pascal speaks of the centrality of Jesus Christ, the ground of our faith:

> "Jesus Christ is the object of all things, the centre towards which all things tend. Whoever knows him knows the reason for everything."[34]

Have you ever thought of it this way before, that Christ is the reason for everything? What a motivation for knowing Him better!

This lesson requires your diligent attention as we look at one of the most challenging passages in Scripture (Hebrews 6:4-6). Christians do not always agree on the interpretation so we need to extend grace to one another. We will approach the text with a solid hermeneutic, meaning a solid set of interpretive principles (see Appendix C, About Hermeneutics). Our goal is to stay true to what Scripture teaches so we may grow more mature in our faith.

Part II: Studying Scripture

Read Hebrews 5:11-14

1. Elementary Teachings: Milk

a) A problem has become evident with regard to the readers. In v. 11, why does the author interrupt his discussion of Jesus' obedience and high priesthood in the order of Melchizedek?

b) A diet of *physical milk* might be appropriate for very young children but it provides inadequate nutrition for adults. Similarly, a diet of *spiritual milk* is inadequate for mature believers. What happens when a believer feeds only on spiritual milk?

5:12 _____

5:13 _____

2. Mature Teachings: Solid Food

a) What is the earliest Bible lesson you recall learning? How well did you understand it?

b) Although it is desirable to have a child-like, whole-hearted faith in Christ, it does not honor God to remain childishly ignorant and immature in faith. The readers' failure to learn and grow in faith has nothing to do with their age, intelligence, or ability to hear physically. They instead have a moral failure, a heart issue. Spiritual immaturity and maturity are contrasted below.

Growing Toward Maturity

	Spiritual Immaturity (v. 11-13)	Spiritual Maturity (v. 12, 14)
Diet?	Spiritual milk	Spiritual solid food
For whom?	Childish, infant-like believers	Mature believers
Results?	Dull of hearing, slow to learn, unskilled in righteousness	Trained by constant practice, can distinguish good from evil
Next step?	Relearn elementary principles	Ready to teach the basics

---

Looking at the above chart, why is it morally imperative for believers to seek solid food? Which side of the chart best describes your current status?

c) The author refuses to re-teach basic doctrine and expects his readers to be ready to learn about Jesus' priesthood in the order of Melchizedek. How can Christians today find a church that offers this kind of mature teaching, for the benefit of their ongoing spiritual growth?

d) Too often Christians expect to be entertained by a pastor's sermon. They are critical if they think the pastor is dull of speech, but they forget that God is more concerned about His worshipers being dull of hearing and slow to learn. How can we get better at listening well to sermons? What can we do to prepare ourselves ahead of time?

Read Hebrews 6:1-3

3.   Confident Faith

a)   Our Bibles tell us to go or press on to maturity but the original Greek uses the passive voice, "Let us *be carried* on to maturity." Our active participation is still implied, but the Holy Spirit carries us so we can better pursue maturity. How do you feel knowing you do not have to do this on your own strength?

b)   List six foundational teachings the author expects his readers to understand.[35] Taken in pairs, these ABC's represent three essential areas: inner faith, external rituals, and church doctrine. Which of these elementary topics could you teach and which have you been a bit sluggish about learning?

6:1   _____

_____

6:2   _____

_____

_____

_____

c)   In v. 3, what phrase indicates that we need to rely on God's help in understanding difficult Christian doctrine such as the upcoming teaching on the priesthood of Melchizedek?

Read Hebrews 6:4-6

4.   Unbelievers Fall Away

a)   Here we come to one of the most difficult passages in the Bible. This passage is merely one sentence long but has provoked volumes of discussion. We will begin by noting that the author has been speaking about himself and his readers as we, us, and you. What different pronouns indicate the author is now referring to someone else, not the readers?

b) The identity of those who fell away is unknown. It is possible they were once members of the readers' church and had enjoyed blessings of *common grace* which God bestows on both believers and unbelievers. In v. 4-5, find three verbs (technically participles)[36] that describe some of the ways all people can participate in God's common grace blessings.

c) Read Hebrews 10:34-39. The author describes his believing readers in Hebrews 10 differently than the unbelievers who fell away in Hebrews 6. In addition to common grace blessings, true believers receive blessings of *saving grace*, including faith, salvation, confidence, endurance, perseverance, reward, fulfilled promises, and heavenly possessions. In v. 39, what will happen to unbelievers? What about the author and the believing readers?

d) This study agrees with scholars who conclude that those who fell away in Hebrews 6 were never true believers. They enjoyed God's common grace blessings and saw His saving work, but fell away into apostasy. How were they like the Israelites in the wilderness (see Hebrews 3:8-12)?

e) Read John 6:64-71. The apostle Judas is someone who experienced God's common grace blessings and witnessed God's saving work, but fell away into apostasy, revealing that he never truly believed. In v. 65, what necessary element for his conversion was missing?[37]

f) Read Romans 6:9. Even if unbelievers could be brought to repentance,[38] they would then need a second atonement since they rejected the first one. Why is it impossible for Jesus Christ to provide a second atonement?

5. True Believers Cannot Lose Salvation

a) Many Christians suppose that true believers can lose and regain their salvation, perhaps numerous times, but this passage does not support that view. In v. 4-6, what is the possibility of someone being restored to repentance after having fallen away?

b) Read John 10:27-29. What does Jesus say about true believers losing salvation?

c) Read John 6:37-40 and Romans 8:30. What is the inevitable destiny of true believers?

d) Read Romans 6:3-14. True believers are united to Jesus Christ. They participate in His suffering, death, and resurrection symbolically through their baptism. It is impossible for true believers to unparticipate in Christ's body once they are joined to it. In other words, true believers cannot lose their salvation. Anyone who falls away was never saved and united to Christ in the first place. How should union with Christ affect the way we live?

Read Hebrews 6:7-12

6. The Evidence of True Belief

In v. 7-8, the author provides a parable to illustrate the preceding difficult passage. The imagery comes from Isaiah 5:1-7 where God's vineyard, Israel, fails to produce good fruit. The land receives rain and at first there is no vegetation to reveal what kind of land it is. Eventually, though, the vegetation reveals what the land is really like.

Land = God's people (those who profess faith, both believers and unbelievers).

Rain = God's common grace blessings (God's word and the Spirit's work).

Similarly, God's people receive God's common grace blessings. At first there is nothing in their lives to reveal whether they are true believers. Eventually, though, their lives produce evidence that indicates whether they are true believers or unbelievers.

a) In v. 7, how are mature true believers like the cultivated land? In v. 8, how are unbelievers who fall away similar to the worthless land?

b) The author is confident that his readers are not like the people who fell away in v. 4-6. In v. 9, what "better things" do the readers have?

c) In v. 10, which evidence of saving grace is especially noticeable in the readers' lives: faith, hope, or love?

d) In v. 11-12, what attitude should they have about the other two evidences? This is true for us as well.

e)   In 6:12, the Greek word for sluggish or lazy is the same word translated dull or slow in 5:11, forming an *inclusio* or enclosure around the author's long warning. He has set apart the warning for emphasis. Pay attention!

Part III: Personal Application and Growth

Today's lesson points to several important truths that apply to our personal lives. Allow these truths to penetrate your mind, soften your heart, deepen your faith and affect your behavior to help you continually grow in Christ.

1.   Believers can strengthen their faith by studying mature Christian teaching.

This week make a plan for the coming year to read some classics of the faith that expound Biblical principles in practical terms. You might begin with C.S. Lewis' apologetic, *Mere Christianity,* or Saint Augustine's famous prayer diary, *Confessions.* What obstacles might interfere with carrying out your reading plan? How will you overcome any obstacles?

2.   An ongoing desire to seek mature teaching gives us assurance of salvation.

Talk to mature believers in your church who have studied the Bible for years with an abiding hunger and thirst to know Christ more. Ask how their repeated study of Scripture has deepened their assurance of faith. What inspires you about their responses? How will you imitate their diligence?

3.   Rituals and church doctrine are essential companions to our faith life.

Start today to learn the oldest creed of the Christian faith, the Apostles' Creed. The first eight articles deal with the triune God and the last four articles refer to believers. Each day ponder and memorize two of the Creed's brief articles, beginning with the two below. The entire creed is printed in the Endnotes.[39]

(1) *I believe in God the Father Almighty, Maker of heaven and earth,*

(2) *And in Jesus Christ, His only Son, our Lord*

Part IV: Closing Devotion

by Charles Spurgeon

Believer, if you would enjoy full assurance of faith, under the blessed Spirit's influence and assistance do what Scripture tells you, "be all the more diligent" (II Peter 1:10). Give diligence if you want assurance, for lukewarmness and doubting very naturally go hand in hand.

Give diligence to your *faith*, depending on Christ and on Christ alone. Give diligent heed to your *courage* that you may, with a consciousness of right, go on boldly. Study well the Scriptures and get *knowledge*, for a knowledge of doctrine will tend very much to confirm faith. Try to understand God's Word; let it dwell in your heart richly.

Practice *temperance* outside your body and within. Add to this, by God's Holy Spirit, *patience* to endure affliction, that you may not murmur or be depressed. Attend to *godliness*; make God's glory your object in life, and seek fellowship with Him. Add *brotherly love* for all the saints, and a *charity* which opens its arms to all people and loves their souls.

When you are adorned with these jewels, and in proportion as you practice these heavenly virtues, you will come to know by clearest evidence your calling and election.[40]

❧ Lesson 10 ❧

Attention! Believe God's Promises

Hebrews 6:13-20

Part I: Setting the Stage

Purpose

This lesson explores the Old Testament proof text supporting the author's warning in the previous lesson to strive for spiritual maturity in order to have assurance of salvation. It is important for us to know, like the patriarch Abraham, that God fulfills His saving promises even when we cannot see how.

Look for the following application points in this lesson:

1. God's promises to Abraham extend to all true believers, the universal church.
2. We have assurance that God keeps His saving promises.
3. Our hope of salvation is anchored in heaven where Jesus lives to intercede for us.

What Is a Covenant?

By pure grace God makes Himself known to humans and invites us to have a loving relationship with Him. Without His reaching out to us we would never know how to find Him or please Him. Throughout history God has chosen to relate to humans through a series of agreements and promises called covenants in Scripture.

God creates the binding provisions of each covenant and His people can accept or reject the provisions but not change them. God does not change the provisions, either, but He can fulfill and replace a covenant. A formal definition of a Biblical covenant is "an unchangeable, divinely imposed legal agreement between God and man that stipulates the conditions of their relationship."[41]

The Abrahamic Covenant

There are several covenants in Scripture. The author of Hebrews focuses on three: the Abrahamic covenant, the Mosaic covenant, and the New Covenant mediated by Jesus Christ. Our current proof text deals with the Abrahamic covenant.

God called Abraham around 2000 B.C. to be the father of a great people set apart for Him in the land of His choosing. God's covenant stipulated His provision of land, descendants, and Abraham's seed being a blessing to the whole world. God swore an oath in order to give extra assurance that He would fulfill His covenant promises. In return, God required His people's faithful obedience to His word.

God's Oath

God makes several oaths in Scripture to assure people that His word will inevitably come to pass. As noted in Lesson 7, three of these oaths are discussed in the book of Hebrews. These three oaths occurred about five hundred years apart at crucial moments in redemptive history, in the times of Abraham, Moses, and David.

We have already read about God's oath during the wilderness rebellion in Moses' time when God swore that unbelievers would never enter His rest. If we think for a minute, we can see how that oath is related to God's prior oath with Abraham. Through Abraham, God vowed to give His people a Promised Land. Then through Moses, God led His people to the Promised Land, vowing that those guilty of covenant disobedience would never enter the land.

Our Sure Inheritance

It is a matter of historical record that God kept His oaths. Initial fulfillment of the Abrahamic covenant came through the physical descendants born to Abraham and their settlement in the land of Canaan.

Longer-term, spiritual, messianic fulfillment of God's covenant promises come through Jesus. Jesus Christ is the Seed of Abraham who is the promised blessing to the world (Galatians 3:16). He continues to bless the world through His body, the church. The true descendants of Abraham are the true believers in all eras, the universal church (Galatians 3:29), whose inherited land is heaven. Believers can be encouraged to know they have inherited the Abrahamic promises and that those promises are fulfilled in Jesus Christ.

Part II: Studying Scripture

Since God's covenant with Abraham is the context for the proof text in this lesson, we will spend some time brushing up on the Abrahamic covenant in Genesis.

First, God told Abram (later called Abraham) to move 1,500 miles from the land of Ur in Mesopotamia to the unknown land of Canaan (Genesis 15:7). On the way to Canaan, Abram's father settled the family in Haran in present-day Turkey near Syria (Genesis 11:31). Then God called Abram to continue to Canaan, the land God would show him (Genesis 12:1).

Read Genesis 12:1-7

1. Abram's Call

a) In God's call to Abram we see the structure of the covenant taking shape. Two main elements of the covenant are God's promise to provide land and descendants. In v. 1, what is Abram's responsibility?

b) In v. 4-7, how does Abram respond to God's command? What do you suppose were some of the difficulties Abram faced? What does Abram's obedience reveal about his faith?

Read Genesis 15:1-6

It would be hard to overstate the importance of God's covenant with Abram. It was a major turning point in the unfolding of God's redemptive plan for the world. God's purpose was to create a people set apart for Himself in a land set apart for Himself, so that through His elect people God might bless the whole world. God ultimately worked out His redemptive plan through the true Seed of Abraham, Jesus Christ.

2. Abram's Faith

a) In v. 2-3, what is Abram's concern with regard to God's promise of descendants?

b) In v. 4-5, how does God reassure Abram?

c) In v. 6, what is Abram's response to God? How does God react to Abram's response? Here we see that justification is by faith alone, for Abram did no works to earn righteousness and he believed God's saving word without seeing evidence of fulfillment.

Read Genesis 15:7-11, 17-18

3. The Ratification Ceremony

a) In v. 8, what is Abram's concern with regard to God's promise of land?

b) God reassures Abram by ratifying the covenant in a ceremony using sacrificial animals that were ceremonially clean. The intrusive and unclean birds of prey represented nations that would seek to destroy Abram and his descendants. In v. 11, what is Abram's responsibility with regard to protecting his promised inheritance?

c) In v. 17, the cloud and fire represent God's presence passing between the animal parts. It was customary for parties of an ancient covenant to pass between torn animals to ratify a covenant, signifying they were to be treated the same way if they violated the covenant. Why do you think God took this oath?

Read Genesis 22:15-18

4. Confirming the Covenant

In Genesis 17, God confirmed His covenant with Abraham. He changed Abram's name to Abraham and Sarai's name to Sarah, promised them an heir, promised to be their God, and ordained the rite of circumcision as a sign of the covenant.

Here in Genesis 22, God confirms the covenant again. This is the proof text quoted in Hebrews. It has been years since the covenant ratification ceremony, and Abraham now faces the greatest of all tests to his faith. God orders Abraham to sacrifice his son Isaac, the promised heir and only son of the covenant. Abraham is willing to proceed, trusting that God will resurrect Isaac. At the last moment God provides a substitute sacrifice and spares Isaac.

a) According to Jewish tradition, Isaac was thirty-seven years old when he was nearly sacrificed. The 1st century Jewish historian Josephus says he was twenty-five. In any event, what would the loss of Isaac mean for fulfillment of the covenant promise of descendants?

b) In v. 15-18, it sounds as if God swears to keep His covenant on the basis of Abraham's faithfulness in sacrificing Isaac. However, God is confirming the oath He took at the ratification ceremony decades before Isaac was born. Why do you think Abraham needed to hear God's affirmation at this time?

c) In v. 18, God confirms His covenant promise that the whole world will be blessed by Abraham's seed. How does the episode with Isaac foreshadow or prepare us for the coming of God's Son, Jesus Christ, the Seed of Abraham?

Read Hebrews 6:13-20

5. God's Oath

At last we are ready for our current passage in Hebrews. The author's proof text focuses on God's covenant promise of descendants to Abraham, "I will surely bless you, and I will surely multiply your offspring..." (Genesis 22:17). The promise will inevitably be fulfilled because God took an oath.

a) Regarding oaths, why do witnesses today take an oath before giving testimony in court? By whom do witnesses traditionally swear in court? Why are witnesses asked to call upon the highest possible authority to verify their testimony?

b) In v. 13, who is the authority by whom God swears to keep His promises? Why is it impossible for there to be any stronger assurance? How will you learn to trust God's promises more?

c) In v. 15, in one sense Abraham obtained fulfillment of God's promise of descendants through his son Isaac. On the other hand, in what sense was fulfillment of God's promise still in the future?

d) In v. 17, what was the reason God took the oath? Four thousand years later, how does this reason affect you as an heir of the promise?

e) In v. 18, commentators hold various opinions as to the identity of "two unchangeable things." A reasonable view is that the unchangeable things are God's covenant promise and His oath confirming the promise. How are you encouraged by the surety of God's promises?

6. Our Sure Hope Is Anchored

Theologian J. I. Packer points out that Christianity is a religion of hope, a faith that looks forward. He writes about the certainty of our hope:

> "Think of our hope not as a possibility nor yet as a likelihood, but as a guaranteed certainty, because it is a *promised inheritance*. The reason for adopting, in the first-century world, was specifically to have an heir to whom one could bequeath one's goods. So, too, God's adoption of us makes us his heirs, and so guarantees to us, as our right (we might say), the inheritance that he has in store

for us... Our Father's wealth is immeasurable and we are to inherit the entire estate... God's promise to us and his work in us are not going to fail."[42]

a) In v. 19, the author employs a vivid word picture to speak of the certainty of our hope. He says our hope of salvation is anchored in heaven, in the inner place behind the curtain or veil, where Jesus has gone as high priest to prepare the way for us. This hope is not imaginary, wishful thinking, but a sure reality that keeps our souls steady during the storms of life.

An anchor normally reaches down into the invisible waters of the sea to fasten on a rock. Gravity keeps the heavy anchor in place. In the author's metaphor, though, our hope is anchored in the inner places of heaven. It is as if our anchor of hope is secured in heaven on Christ the Rock (I Corinthians 10:4), and God's oath is the rope that connects the anchor to our soul. What do you find startling about the image of an anchor in heaven?

b) Although this is the only place the word anchor appears in Scripture other than the mention of a literal ship anchor in connection with Paul's travels (Acts 27), an anchor was a common representation of hope in New Testament times. Early Christian tombs showed an image of an anchor next to a fish, the symbol for Christ, or an anchor superimposed on a cross. What do you find helpful about the image of an anchor?

c) The chapter closes by bringing us back to the discussion of Melchizedek. The references to Melchizedek at 5:10 and 6:20 form an *inclusio* or enclosure around the warning in Hebrews 6, making it stand out. We are warned to be ready for the upcoming mature teaching on Jesus our King-Priest. It is time for solid food. Pay attention!

Part III: Personal Application and Growth

Today's lesson points to several important truths that apply to our personal lives. Allow these truths to penetrate your mind, soften your heart, deepen your faith and affect your behavior to help you continually grow in Christ.

1. God's promises to Abraham extend to all true believers, the universal church.

One of the promises in the Abrahamic covenant was that the seed of Abraham would bless the whole world. Jesus Christ is the true Seed of Abraham who continues to bless the world through His body, the church. As part of Christ's body, what will you do to be a blessing to someone today?

2. We have assurance that God keeps His saving promises.

This week notice how often people make promises without intending to carry through. Thank the Lord for keeping His word and being faithful in all His saving promises in Christ. What steps will you take to become more reliable at keeping your word?

3. Our hope of salvation is anchored in heaven where Jesus lives to intercede for us.

What practical steps will you take to make the unseen reality of Jesus' intercession in heaven more real to you?

Part IV: Closing Devotion
by Charles Spurgeon

Believer, where lies the secret strength of faith? It lies in the food it feeds on. Faith studies *what* the promise is – an emanation of divine grace, an overflowing of the great heart of God; and faith says, "My God could not have given this promise, except from love and grace; therefore it is quite certain His Word will be fulfilled."

Then faith thinks, "*Who* gave this promise?" Faith remembers that it is God who cannot lie – God omnipotent, God immutable; and therefore concludes with firm conviction that the promise must be fulfilled. Faith remembers *why* the promise was given – namely, for God's glory; and feels perfectly sure that God's glory is safe, and therefore the promise will stand.

Then faith also considers the amazing *work of Christ* as being a clear proof of the Father's intention to fulfill His word. "He who did not spare his own Son but gave him up for us all, how will he not also with him graciously give us all things?" (Romans 8:32)

Moreover, faith looks back upon *the past*. Faith remembers that God never did once fail any of His children. Faith cries, "I never will be led to think He can change and leave His servant now. Hitherto the Lord has helped me, and He will help me still."[43]

❧ Lesson 11 ❦

The Greatest King

Hebrews 7:1-10

Part I: Setting the Stage

Purpose

This lesson studies the mysterious figure of Melchizedek, the great king-priest to whom Jesus Christ is compared in Hebrews. It is important for us to contemplate the person of Melchizedek so that we better understand Jesus' fulfillment of the office of king.

Look for the following application points in this lesson:

1. Jesus perfectly fulfills the office of king.
2. Jesus reigns as a king of righteousness and peace.
3. It is encouraging to know God provides His people with a royal priesthood.

Introducing Melchizedek

Melchizedek (mel-KIH-zeh-deck) is mentioned only twice in the Old Testament. Many Christians are not familiar with him, but he holds the key to understanding Jesus as king and high priest. This is mature teaching for those who want to strengthen their faith.

The name or title Melchizedek is Semitic, indicating he may have descended from Noah's son Shem like Abraham. In fact, Jewish tradition identifies Melchizedek as the revered Shem, an old man in Abraham's time. The Hebrew word *melech* means king and *zedek* means righteousness, so Melchizedek was a king of righteousness. He was also king of Salem, later called Jerusalem. *Salem* is related to the Hebrew word *shalom,* meaning peace, so Melchizedek was a king of peace. His righteousness and peace foreshadow the Messiah (Isaiah 32:1, 17).

In addition to being king, Melchizedek was priest of God Most High (*El Elyon*), the true God worshiped by the patriarchs. The dual role of king and priest was not forbidden by God at that time. Once again, Melchizedek foreshadows the Messiah who was prophesied to be both king and priest (Zechariah 6:12-13).

Abraham Meets Melchizedek

When Abraham (Abram) and his nephew Lot moved to Canaan, the area was controlled by a strong confederacy of kings led by the king of Elam in modern Iran. Several Canaanite vassal states including Sodom and Gomorrah decided to rebel against the confederacy. However, the confederacy soon defeated the rebels, plundering the city of Sodom and carrying off Lot and his possessions.

Hearing of Lot's captivity, Abraham gathered an army and made a daring rescue. On Abraham's way home with the spoils of war, two kings came out to meet him. These kings represent two extremes. One was wicked Bera, the defeated king of Sodom whose city had been plundered. The other was righteous Melchizedek, the peaceful king of Salem who had not gone to war. In the Bible's concise way we are told that Abraham willingly paid homage to Melchizedek and spurned Bera.

The encounter with Melchizedek takes us by surprise, but it does not seem to surprise or intimidate Abraham. It appears that Abraham already knew of Melchizedek, God's righteous and superior king-priest.

The Spiritual Significance

The author of Hebrews unpacks this brief historical encounter and opens our eyes to its spiritual significance. He reasons in the style of a rabbi. One of his central themes is solidarity or representative headship in matters of salvation. Our society tends to emphasize individuality, but the author thinks in terms of solidarity with a group. Although his explanation is not simple, the meaning will unfold if we follow along carefully.

Abraham and his great-grandson Levi represent the Levitical priesthood that descended from them. When Abraham honors Melchizedek, it is as if the Levitical priesthood honors the Melchizedek priesthood, even though the Levitical priesthood was not established until five hundred years later. The order of Melchizedek was therefore always superior to the Levitical order.

The idea of solidarity or representative headship is actually central to the Christian faith. Adam was the representative head of all humanity and when he sinned all who belonged to him fell with him. Christ is the representative head of the church and His atonement saves all who belong to Him. It should encourage us to know Christ represents and saves all of His people.

Part II: Studying Scripture

Read Genesis 14:17-24

Theologian R. C. Sproul reminds us that the events of the Bible, like the mysterious episode of Melchizedek, are solidly grounded in linear history:

> "From the opening chapters of Genesis to the end of the book of Revelation, the entire dynamic of redemption takes place within the broader setting of real space and time, of concrete history... redemption is inseparably tied to the reality of the historical context in which it takes place."[44]

1. The Historical Account

a) Two Canaanite kings met Abram (Abraham) on his way home from war. In v. 18-20, what did Melchizedek, the king-priest of Salem on Mount Moriah, offer Abram in gratitude for victory? How did Abram respond?

b) In v. 21-24, what did Bera, the king of Sodom, offer Abram and how did Abram respond?

c)   Why did Abram honor Melchizedek and reject Bera (see Genesis 13:13)?

d)   Melchizedek showed superiority over Abram by mediating between Abram and God. Melchizedek spoke for God and blessed Abram; then he spoke for Abram and blessed God. By accepting Melchizedek's mediation, Abram acknowledged Melchizedek's superiority. What does this tell you about Abram's character?

2.   A Theophany or Type of Christ?

Some think Melchizedek was a visible manifestation of God (a theophany) appearing as the pre-incarnate Christ. Others, including this study, consider him a historical figure presented in Scripture as a type pointing to Christ. Since both views have merit, we should graciously acknowledge that in the end Melchizedek remains something of a mystery.

a)   The historical narrative in Genesis 14 presents Melchizedek as a known political figure with a name, title, and kingdom. These details distinguish him from theophanies where an unknown stranger appears from nowhere. How do we know that Melchizedek's territory, the area of Mount Moriah, was known to Abram apart from this event (see Genesis 22:2)?

b)   Melchizedek is not identified as God, LORD, or an angel of the LORD. This sets him apart from theophanies where a stranger is identified by such a title. What title does Scripture give the strangers in the following theophanies?

Abraham meets three men (Genesis 18:1-2):   _____
Jacob wrestles with a man (Genesis 32:24-28):   _____
Samson's mother meets a man (Judges 13:3, 6):   _____

Read Hebrews 7:1-3

3. Understanding the Account

a) There is a saying about the Old and New Testaments, "The New is in the Old concealed; the Old is in the New revealed." The author of Hebrews explains the spiritual significance of the Genesis narrative for us. In v. 1, what was the reason Melchizedek went out to meet Abram?

b) The author leaves out certain details in the re-telling, presumably because they are not significant. This focuses our attention on the remaining details. What does he say about Abram's encounter with Bera, the king of Sodom?

c) What does the author say about Melchizedek's provision of bread and wine to Abram? The expression "bread and wine" simply meant a full meal of food and drink (see its use in Judges 19:19). There is no indication that the meal in Genesis represented communion or held any theological significance.

4. A Different Kind of Priesthood

a) In v. 3, the phrase "without father or mother or genealogy" is not to be taken literally to mean Melchizedek was supernatural and therefore the pre-incarnate Christ. We run into a problem if Melchizedek is deemed to be Christ prior to His humanity, for Christ was not a priest prior to His humanity. Melchizedek the priest could not be the pre-incarnate Christ who was not a priest.

It does no good to argue we are getting a glimpse of the future incarnate Christ as priest, for then He would have human parents and genealogy.

The phrase rather means there was no written record of Melchizedek's ancestry. The phrase emphasizes the difference between Melchizedek's priesthood and the Levitical priesthood, a major theme in Hebrews. What did the law require of Levitical priests (see Ezra 2:62)? No such written records were required of Melchizedek and Jesus since their priesthood was not established by law and had no inherited positions.

b) Again in v. 3, the phrase "having neither beginning of days nor end of life" is not to be taken literally to mean Melchizedek was immortal. The phrase emphasizes the difference between the Melchizedek priesthood and the Levitical priesthood. What did the law say about the length of a Levitical priest's term (see Numbers 8:24-25)? Unlike Levitical priests, Melchizedek's priestly term did not end upon his retirement or death.

c) The author says Melchizedek resembled (literally, "was made like") the Son of God. The use of a simile is persuasive evidence that Melchizedek was not Christ, but a type whom God intended to point to Christ. Notice the resemblances summarized below. The last item is arguably the most important one for us.

How Melchizedek Resembles Jesus Christ

7:1   Melchizedek is a king-priest and he gives priestly blessing.
7:2   He receives homage and tithes.
       He reigns in righteousness and peace.
7:3   He has no genealogy to qualify him as a Levitical priest.
       His priesthood lives forever.

Why does our salvation depend on a priesthood that never ends?

Read Hebrews 7:4-10

5. Melchizedek Is Greater Than Abraham

One of the author's techniques is to present a great person in order to show that someone else is greater by comparison. In this passage the patriarch Abraham is great, but Melchizedek is greater. Accordingly, the Levitical priesthood that descended from Abraham is great, but Melchizedek's priesthood is greater. Here is a simple timeline to give perspective as we work our way through this complex passage:

2000 B.C.	1500 B.C.	1000 B.C.	500 B.C.	A.D. 1
| Levi	|	|	|	|
Abraham meets Melchizedek	Moses sets up the Levitical priesthood	David writes Psalm 110		Jesus Christ

a) In v. 5, what gave Levitical priests the right to collect tithes from their fellow Israelites, even though all Israelites were equally descended from the great Abraham?

b) It was stunning that Abraham, a man with God's covenant promises, paid tithes to a priest who did not have those promises. Melchizedek was not a descendant of Abraham and had no right to collect tithes by law. Yet in v. 6-7, why did paying a tithe prove that Abraham saw Melchizedek as an authoritative representative of God with superior status?

c) In v. 8, on one hand, inferior Levitical priests were "mortal men" whose terms came to an end, proved by written records. In contrast, there was no record that the term of the superior priest Melchizedek ended when he died, so symbolically he is said to "live." He lives in the sense that his priesthood is permanent. The priest who literally lives forever in the order of Melchizedek is Jesus Christ. Who testified to this (see Hebrews 5:5-6, quoting Psalm 110:4)?

d) Levi was the founder and representative head of the tribe of Levites. In v. 9-10, in a sense Levi *received* tithes because his descendants, the Levitical priests, received tithes. Levi and his descendants also *paid* tithes earlier through Levi's great-grandfather Abraham, for Levi was in Abraham's loins or seed when Abraham met Melchizedek. Therefore, through their representatives Levi and Abraham, the Levitical priesthood had always honored and submitted to the Melchizedek priesthood. How well do you follow this?

6. Jesus Is Greater Than Melchizedek

When the author deals with the office of king, we may find it odd that he compares Jesus to Melchizedek, a Canaanite king, rather than David, the greatest king of Israel. Melchizedek must somehow be greater than David.

a) Read II Samuel 7:16, 8:15. There is no doubt that David was a great king despite his sinful shortcomings. David was a man after God's own heart more than any other king in the history of Israel and Judah. What was God's covenant promise to David? The Davidic covenant has been fulfilled by Jesus Christ, the enthroned Messiah, the Son of David.

b) Read Zechariah 6:12-13. The prophet Zechariah foretold that the Branch or Messiah would be both priest and king. The role of king-priest was greater than king alone. Here is the key to why Jesus is compared to Melchizedek rather than David. David was a great king, but Melchizedek was a king-priest. With regard to the fulfillment of messianic prophecies like Zechariah's, what did Jesus say (see Luke 24:44)?

111

c) Jesus Christ is superior to Melchizedek because Jesus is the Son of God, the king and high priest who lives forever. The significance of this truth will be explored more fully in the next lesson.

Part III: Personal Application and Growth

Today's lesson points to several important truths that apply to our personal lives. Allow these truths to penetrate your mind, soften your heart, deepen your faith and affect your behavior to help you continually grow in Christ.

1. Jesus perfectly fulfills the office of king.

Jesus rules over all nations and leaders, whether they acknowledge His universal reign or not. Which specific leaders will you pray for each day this week, asking God to turn their hearts to our Lord Jesus so they will lead and make decisions in recognition and submission to His perfect, loving authority?

2. Jesus reigns as a king of righteousness and peace.

What practical steps will you take to live in increased harmony with your neighbors as a tangible example to them of how to live as a citizen of Christ's righteous and peaceful kingdom?

3. It is encouraging to know God provides His people with a royal priesthood.

Christianity is unique in teaching that God reaches down to people to provide salvation, unlike religions where people must try to reach up to God and earn the right to be reconciled to Him. With this in mind, how will you answer someone who wrongly says all religions are basically teaching the same thing?

Part IV: Closing Devotion
by Charles Spurgeon

Believer, our Lord Jesus was once crucified, dead and buried, but now sits upon the throne of glory. The highest place that heaven affords is His by undisputed right.

Look up, believer, to Jesus now; let the eye of your faith behold Him with many crowns upon His head; and remember that you will one day be like Him, when you shall see Him as He is; you shall not be so great as He is, but still you shall, in a measure, share the same honors, and enjoy the same happiness and the same dignity which He possesses.

Be content to live unknown for a little while, and to walk your weary way through the fields of poverty, or up the hills of affliction; for by-and-by you shall reign with Christ, for He has made us to be kings and priests unto God, and we shall reign forever and ever.

Oh!, wonderful thought for the children of God! We have Christ for our glorious representative in heaven's courts *now*, and soon He will come and receive us to Himself, to be with Him, to behold His glory, and to share His joy.[45]

❧ Lesson 12 ❧

A King-Priest Forever

Hebrews 7:11-28

Part I: Setting the Stage

Purpose

This lesson considers Jesus' role as high priest forever in the order of Melchizedek. The Melchizedek priesthood is far superior to the Levitical priesthood. It is important for us to grasp the significance of Jesus being a king who represents God and at the same time a high priest who represents us. Jesus Christ the King-Priest is forever our Lord-Savior.

Look for the following application points in this lesson:

1. Jesus Christ is forever our perfect King and High Priest, our Lord and Savior.
2. Jesus Christ is the only way of salvation.
3. We have assurance that Christ saves because God Himself has promised it.

One Plan

Two thousand years before Christ's birth, God took important steps toward implementing His ultimate plan of salvation:

- God established a permanent priesthood through Melchizedek.
- God established a permanent elect people through Abraham.

The written record in Genesis and Hebrews assures us that these two imposing figures, Melchizedek and Abraham, together were an integral part of God's saving plan. Scripture tells us that Melchizedek served as priest to Abraham and Abraham submitted to Melchizedek, acknowledging that Melchizedek was his superior and God's representative. Eventually God's plan of salvation was fulfilled in Jesus Christ, the descendant of Abraham who became a high priest in the order of Melchizedek.

Two Priesthoods

The Melchizedek Priesthood

God set up the permanent, royal, priestly order of Melchizedek around the time He called Abraham to be father of His chosen people. Since Melchizedek's priestly term did not end upon his death, the Melchizedek priesthood has no end. In the fullness of time, Jesus Christ came into the world to become high priest in the order of Melchizedek.

The Levitical Priesthood

God graciously provided a second priesthood to serve the needs of His people until the arrival of Jesus Christ. This temporary priesthood was the Levitical or Aaronic priesthood. The Levitical priesthood was established by Mosaic Law after the Exodus (around 1446 B.C.) and it ended in A.D. 70. Moses' brother Aaron from the tribe of Levi was the first high priest, and all other priests were to come from Aaron's line.

The two priesthoods co-existed for about 1,500 years. The priesthood of Jesus Christ in the order of Melchizedek fulfilled and replaced the Levitical priesthood, making it obsolete. The true descendants of Abraham, the universal church, come to God through their high priest Jesus Christ. We have assurance that our salvation is secure because Christ's kingdom and priesthood live forever, unlike the Levitical priesthood.

Three Oaths

This lesson looks at God's third oath whereby He swears Jesus will be "a priest forever after the order of Melchizedek" (Hebrews 7:17). God's three oaths in the book of Hebrews work together to give us full assurance of salvation, as summarized below.

God's Oaths

Oath #1

God will keep His saving covenant promises to Abraham (Genesis 15:17; 22:16). Abraham's true spiritual descendants, the church, inherit the saving promises (Galatians 3:7, 29). Application: *God will inevitably fulfill His promises of salvation.*

Oath #2

God will not allow the unbelieving Israelites in the wilderness to enter His rest in Canaan (Numbers 14:22). Unbelievers in every era will fail to enter God's eternal rest and presence. Application: *Unbelievers never receive salvation.*

Oath #3

God makes Jesus Christ a high priest forever in the order of Melchizedek (Psalm 110:4). Jesus is our perfect high priest who always lives to make intercession for us, thereby ensuring our eternal salvation. Application: *Believers always receive salvation.*

Part II: Studying Scripture

Read Hebrews 7:11-14

1. The Need for a Superior High Priest

An important theme in Hebrews is that the Levitical priesthood and Mosaic Law were never meant to continue forever. They were instituted for a limited purpose and time as the means by which God dealt with national Israel. God's people ultimately needed a superior high priest whose priesthood would never end, fulfilled in Jesus Christ. The old system came to a final end in A.D. 70.

a) In v. 11, what point does the author make about the inadequacy of the Levitical or Aaronic priesthood? How would you answer the author's rhetorical question?

b) Mosaic Law established the Levitical priesthood and the Levitical priesthood administered the Mosaic Law. In v. 12, if there were to be a change concerning the inadequate Levitical priesthood, what would be necessary?

c) Levitical priests by law had to come from the line of Aaron within the tribe of Levi. In v. 13-14, why did this requirement disqualify Jesus from being a Levitical priest? We can see there had to be a different priesthood sanctioned by God in order for Jesus to serve.

Read Hebrews 7:15-22

2. God's Oath

a) In v. 17, the author quotes a proof text from Psalm 110. Earlier he used this proof text to show that both Christ and the high priest Aaron were appointed to their positions by God (Hebrews 5:6). Now he uses the proof text to contrast the fact that Aaron's descendants inherit their priestly position under the law, while Christ is a priest based on an indestructible life.

Commentators are divided about what an "indestructible life" means in v. 16. It could refer to the resurrection of the *human* Jesus who would never be destroyed again. Or it could mean the immortality of the *divine* Son of God who could not die. Which of these two explanations makes the most sense to you? Why? Either way, since Jesus lives forever He is qualified to fulfill a priesthood that lasts forever.

b) In v. 18, how does the author describe the "former commandment," meaning the Levitical priesthood?

c) In v. 19, what does the author say about the "better hope," meaning the Melchizedek priesthood?

d) God was the one who made the law concerning the priesthood and He was the only one with the authority to change it in the sense of fulfilling and replacing it. In v. 20-21, how does God ensure that Jesus will be a permanent priest in the order of Melchizedek?

e) In Lesson 7 it was pointed out that God's oath ensures something will inevitably happen. There are no contingencies that will change the possibility of its happening. In v. 22, what is the result of God's oath?

Read Psalm 110:1-4

3. Predicted Long Ago

a) The replacement of the Levitical priesthood should not have been a surprise to anyone, for it was announced by God through David's Psalm 110 a thousand years earlier. Psalm 110 was a coronation psalm, possibly written by David when he conquered Jerusalem to make it his capital. With regard to Jerusalem, what did David have in common with Melchizedek?

b) Under the law David could not be both king and priest like Melchizedek, but he looked forward to the day when his descendant, the Messiah, would be enthroned forever as a priest in the order of Melchizedek. In v. 1, how does God (LORD) ensure the kingship of the Messiah (Lord)?

c) In v. 4, how does God ensure the priesthood of the Messiah?

d) The kingship of the Messiah means Jesus Christ is our Lord. He is in control of everything in the universe, protects and provides for us, and has authority over our lives. In addition, the priesthood of the Messiah means Jesus Christ is our Savior. His blood sacrifice and ongoing priestly intercession are the means by which He accomplishes our salvation. What do you most appreciate about Jesus Christ, our royal high priest, our Lord and Savior?

Read Hebrews 7:23-28

4. Our Perfect High Priest

What are some of the ways Jesus is qualified to serve as our perfect royal high priest? (Note that Jesus' being separated from sinners means He is sinless, not isolated.)

7:24 _____

7:25 _____

7:26 _____

7:27 _____

7:28 _____

5. Able to Save

a) Verse 25 is the central message of Hebrews. Rephrase the following four reasons we can be encouraged to keep the faith:

Jesus saves to the uttermost: _____

He saves those who draw near to God through Him: _____

_____

Jesus always lives: _____

He intercedes for believers: _____

b) Think for a moment about the statement that Jesus Christ saves those who draw near to God "through Him." There is no other way of salvation. Why do you suppose some people wrongly think they do not need Christ?

c) Theologian R. C. Sproul warns that asking why God is so narrow-minded as to provide only one way of salvation implies a serious accusation that God has not done enough for our redemption. However, God has done plenty:

> "Suppose this Son of God were rejected, slandered, mocked, tortured, and murdered... Suppose this God offered to His Son's murderers total amnesty, complete forgiveness, transcendent peace that comes with the cleansing of all guilt, victory over death and an eternal life of complete felicity... In light of the universal rebellion against God, the issue is not why is there only one way, by *why is there any way at all?*"[46]

How will you answer critics who claim that one way of salvation is not enough?

d) Read John 14:6; Acts 4:12; and I John 5:12. What is Scripture's testimony regarding the only way to salvation and eternal life?

6. Assurance of Salvation

Theologian John Murray speaks about *implicit* assurance of faith that is planted in our hearts upon conversion. This feeling is given by the Holy Spirit to confirm the truth of Jesus Christ deep within us. Murray says we also have *explicit* assurance, an awareness of the implications of our new status in Christ. This explicit assurance is meant to grow over time. We must not allow immaturity and sin to keep us from developing full explicit assurance:

> "Assurance is cultivated, not through special duties or counsels of perfection but through faithful and diligent use of the means of grace and devotion to the duties which devolve upon us in the family, the church, and the world. The means of grace are the Word, the sacraments, and prayer."[47]

a) Think about Murray's distinction between implicit and explicit assurances of faith. What could go wrong if we expect only our initial feeling of assurance at conversion to sustain us throughout life?

b) How will you be more diligent at developing an explicit assurance of faith through Bible study? Attending worship services? The Lord's Supper? Prayer? How will your assurance of faith deepen as a result of carrying out your duties to family, church, and world with devotion?

Part III: Personal Application and Growth

Today's lesson points to several important truths that apply to our personal lives. Allow these truths to penetrate your mind, soften your heart, deepen your faith and affect your behavior to help you continually grow in Christ.

1. Jesus Christ is forever our perfect King and High Priest, our Lord and Savior.

What will you do starting today to submit to Jesus' lordship over your life in an area you have been reluctant to turn over to Him before?

2.   Jesus Christ is the only way of salvation.

The next time you hear someone criticize Christianity for being exclusive, how will your response convey love for a world that is lost without Christ? Why would it be unloving to keep the news of the only way of salvation to yourself?

3.   We have assurance that Christ saves because God Himself has promised it.

The author of Hebrews has spent seven chapters exploring the truth that Jesus Christ is fully divine, fully human, and the perfect fulfillment of prophet, priest, and king. These doctrines reassure us that Christ is all-powerful, all-wise, and all-good. He is able and willing to save us in accordance with God's promises.

Take a look at the application points at the ends of Lessons 1-12 (see the complete list in Appendix A). Note several points that were new to you or personally meaningful. In what specific ways has your assurance of salvation been strengthened by studying Hebrews so far? What challenges this week will you handle differently because of your stronger assurance and faith in Christ?

Congratulations on reaching the halfway point in this study! You will find even more encouragement to keep the faith in the upcoming second half.

Part IV: Closing Devotion

by Charles Spurgeon

Believer, how can we ever grieve God by doubting His upholding grace? It is contrary to every promise of God's precious Word that you should ever be forgotten or left to perish. If it could be so, where would be the truth of Christ's words, "I give them [my sheep] eternal life, and they will never perish, and no one will snatch them out of my hand"? (John 10:28)

Where would be the doctrines of grace? They would all be disproved if one child of God should perish. Where would be the veracity of God, His honor, His power, His grace, His covenant, His oath, if any of those for whom Christ has died, and who have put their trust in Him, should nevertheless be cast away?

Remember it is sinful to doubt His Word where He has promised you that you shall never perish. Let the eternal life within you express itself in confident rejoicing.

> "The gospel bears my spirit up;
> A faithful and unchanging God
> Lays the foundation of my hope
> In oaths, and promises, and blood."[48]

SECTION III

JESUS CHRIST'S SUPERIOR

PRIESTHOOD

❧ Lesson 13 ❦

Mediator of the New Covenant

Hebrews 8:1-7

Part I: Setting the Stage

Purpose

The next several lessons will consider Jesus Christ's superior priesthood in terms of His superior covenant, sanctuary, and sacrifice. We will start with Christ's role as mediator of the new covenant. It is important for us to appreciate the superiority and finality of Christ's work in securing the new covenant of grace for our salvation.

Look for the following application points in this lesson:

1. Jesus Christ is the mediator of the new covenant of grace.
2. Jesus Christ is the only person who could perfectly fulfill the role of mediator.
3. Our Mediator is a just King and merciful High Priest.

A Brief Review

As we begin the second half of this study guide, let's briefly think about the immense depth and breadth of material covered so far in Hebrews.

The Person of Christ

The author of Hebrews makes it clear that Jesus Christ is one person with two natures, divine and human (Hebrews 1-2). In His divine nature Christ is the Son of God; He is superior to angels and is God Himself. In His

126

human nature Jesus took on a physical body; He is our compassionate Brother and Savior.

The Work of Christ

Jesus Christ is the promised Messiah who perfectly fulfills the offices of prophet, priest and king (Hebrews 3-7). He is superior to the great prophet Moses, the great high priest Aaron, and the great king-priest Melchizedek. The fact that Christ our royal high priest always lives to make intercession for us in the heavenly sanctuary is the central message of Hebrews, and it is profoundly encouraging.

Christ's Priesthood

Having laid down the foundational doctrines concerning the person and work of Christ, the author now tells us more about Christ's royal priesthood. In particular, he emphasizes Christ's covenant, sanctuary, and sacrifice. Since these aspects are interrelated, a discussion of one will inevitably touch on the others in the coming lessons.

- The *covenant* sets forth God's promises and conditions for a relationship with Him.
- Christ's perfect *sacrifice* atones for our sin when we fail to meet God's conditions.
- On the basis of His sacrifice, Christ ministers in the *sanctuary* of God's presence so we may draw near to God without fear of condemnation.

It is sometimes asked why the author of Hebrews is so intensely interested in Christ's priesthood. Perhaps it is because the priesthood is the office that provides a way for us to be heard by God and reconciled to Him. The offices of prophet and king represent God to us, but our heavenly high priest takes our prayers to God and intercedes for us. Since God has provided His beloved Son to be our representative high priest, we have assurance that God knows, loves, and hears us.

The question of whether God cares is one of the most enduring questions of the human experience. When we are struck by disaster, crime, illness, loss, and other discouraging circumstances, even the strongest believer may cry out to know if God cares. The book of Hebrews reminds us that the answer is always a resounding Yes! God cares about His people and has made provision for their eternal salvation in Christ. We can be encouraged to keep the faith because we know we are forgiven and never forgotten.

The Perfect Mediator

In Lesson 10 a covenant was defined as "an unchangeable, divinely imposed legal agreement between God and man that stipulates the conditions of their relationship."[49] Moses mediated the old covenant, the Mosaic Law, given by God. Mosaic Law established the Levitical priesthood, and the Levitical priesthood administered Mosaic Law.

When Jesus came into the world, God appointed Him to be the perfect mediator of a superior new covenant of grace that fulfilled and replaced the old covenant of law. The old covenant's Levitical priesthood was no longer needed because Jesus Christ is a high priest forever in the order of Melchizedek. The perfect new covenant mediated by Christ will never end or be replaced.

Part II: Studying Scripture

Read Hebrews 8:1

1. Jesus, Our High Priest

a) The first word of this chapter in the original Greek is "main thing." The author pauses a moment to summarize the main point of the previous chapter, namely that we have a perfect high priest. Looking back, how did the author describe our high priest (see Hebrews 7:24-26)?

b) In v. 1, what else do we learn about our high priest?

c) Jesus is contrasted with Levitical high priests who performed duties while standing, not sitting. Perhaps the image of Christ being seated symbolizes His finished work on the cross as opposed to the unfinished work of Levitical priests. We should not take the image of Christ being seated too literally, though. For example, describe Jesus' posture in heaven in the verses below:

Stephen's vision (Acts 7:55-56): _____

John's vision (Revelation 2:1): _____

2. Jesus, Our King

a) "Seated at the right hand of the throne" is an expression that signifies a kingly function. It implies a position of honor that entails exaltation, power and authority. Being seated at the right hand of the throne of God ("the Majesty") means our high priest Jesus Christ shares God's authority as king. What did the author say earlier to prepare us for this (see Hebrews 1:3b)?

b) God enthroned Christ after Christ's ascension to heaven. Christ's exaltation as king restored the glory He had before His incarnation, and also began a new reign that had not previously existed. Jesus' present role in glory is called His session. What have we already been told about Christ's reign (see Hebrews 1:8 quoting Psalm 45:6-7)?

3. A King-Priest in Heaven

a) Jesus' kingship and priesthood are inter-connected because Jesus' exaltation as king was the reward for completing His saving work. What did Jesus do to earn exaltation (see Philippians 2:8-9)?

b) In general terms, a king was to administer justice on behalf of God, while a priest was to secure mercy from God for the people. What tends to happen when there is not enough justice in society? What about when there is not enough mercy?

c) Based on your personality and life experience, do you find it more reassuring to know that Christ is just or that He is merciful? Why?

d) Amazingly, in Jesus Christ we have both justice and mercy mediated perfectly by the same person. How will you learn to appreciate both qualities in our heavenly king-priest, Jesus Christ?

e) In what ways will your increased appreciation make you better equipped to spread the good news of Jesus Christ to people who have different needs for justice and mercy than you do?

Read Hebrews 8:2-5

4. A Superior Sanctuary and Sacrifice

a) The Temple and palace were located in separate places in Jerusalem. What would this separation symbolize with regard to the earthly roles of priest and king?

b) What does it affirm about Jesus when we read that the priestly sanctuary and kingly throne are located in the same place in heaven?

c) In v. 2 and 5, what is superior about the heavenly sanctuary compared to the earthly sanctuary (the Tabernacle or Temple)?

d) In v. 3, what is the "something" that our high priest, Jesus Christ, offers as a sacrifice (see Hebrews 7:27)?

e) In v. 4, if Jesus were on earth rather than in heaven, why would He not be allowed to be a Levitical priest according to the law (see Hebrews 7:13-14)?

f) Jesus could not serve in the earthly sanctuary, but He serves in the superior heavenly sanctuary. If there were no heavenly sanctuary where Jesus, our high priest, could serve on the basis of His sacrifice, our salvation would be incomplete. How would you explain the importance of the connection between sanctuary and sacrifice in your own words?

Read Hebrews 8:6-7

5. A Superior Covenant

Moses was mediator of the old covenant given by God. The old covenant of Mosaic Law was "holy and righteous and good" for the purpose for which it was given (Romans 7:12), but it was limited and temporary. God used the law to guide national Israel, establish the Levitical priesthood, and prepare His people for salvation in Christ. In the fullness of time God appointed Jesus Christ to mediate a superior new covenant to fulfill and replace the old.

a) The new covenant is better than the old covenant partly because it was made with God's oath and is guaranteed forever by Christ our mediator. In v. 6, what is another reason the new covenant is better? This reason will be explored in more detail in the next lesson.

b) We tend to forget how radical it was for the author of Hebrews to suggest that the old covenant had been replaced by the new covenant in Christ. In round numbers, how many years had God's people been living under Mosaic Law? (Hint: The Law was put in place from the time of the Exodus, perhaps around 1446 B.C., until the destruction of Jerusalem in A.D. 70.)

c) The old covenant had its limitations and faults from the beginning. It could not give people permanent access to God, empower sinful people to obey God, nor cleanse their guilty consciences. If you had lived in the time of the old covenant, which of these limitations would have distressed you most?

d) In v. 7, what became necessary?

6. A Superior Mediator

a) No one can fully explain exactly how Jesus Christ mediates the covenant of grace between God and His people, but somehow He accomplishes it perfectly. Look up the definition of the verb "mediate" in a dictionary and write it in the space below. Why is it a fitting description of Jesus' work?

b) Jesus has both a human nature that allows Him to perfectly represent us to God, and a divine nature that allows Him to perfectly represent God to us. How does this surpass the role of Moses, mediator of the old covenant?

c) Read I Timothy 2:5. We will always need to approach God through the mediator of His choosing. Who does Paul rightly say is the only Mediator between God and humans?

d) The philosopher Blaise Pascal speaks about the importance of Jesus Christ as our Mediator:

> "We know God only through Jesus Christ. Without this Mediator all communication with God is broken off... To prove Christ we have the prophecies which are solid and palpable proofs. By being fulfilled and proved true by the event, these prophecies show that these truths are certain and thus prove that Jesus is divine.

> "In him and through him, therefore, we know God. Apart from that, without scripture, without original sin, without the necessary mediator who was promised and came, it is impossible to prove absolutely that God exists, or to teach sound doctrine and sound morality."[50]

Why is the person of Jesus Christ the best and only way for us to truly know God? What will you do to know Christ better so you may know God better?

Part III: Personal Application and Growth

Today's lesson points to several important truths that apply to our personal lives. Allow these truths to penetrate your mind, soften your heart, deepen your faith and affect your behavior to help you continually grow in Christ.

1. Jesus Christ is the mediator of the new covenant of grace.

How will you explain to a non-Christian the futility of expecting God to forgive sin outside the new covenant mediated by Christ?

2. Jesus Christ is the only person who could perfectly fulfill the role of mediator.

When we pray in Jesus' name, we approach God the Father by the authorization of the only mediator, Jesus Christ. Our prayers are to be consistent with Jesus' character and will. How will you vary your prayers this week to keep the phrase "in Jesus' name I pray" from becoming a rote formula that loses its meaning? One variation might be, "I pray as Christ would."

3. Our Mediator is a just King and merciful High Priest.

This week try to learn the first eight lines of "The Advocate," an old hymn written in 1863. It has enjoyed resurgence in popularity due to an updated tune, "Before the Throne of God Above." Pay attention to the depth of theology packed into these lyrics:

> "Before the throne of God above
> I have a strong and perfect plea,
> A great High Priest whose name is Love,
> Who ever lives and pleads for me.

My name is graven on His hands,
My name is written on His heart.
I know that while in Heaven He stands,
No tongue can bid me thence depart."[51]

In what particular situations in the coming weeks do you anticipate these words will be an encouragement to you?

Part IV: Closing Devotion
by Charles Spurgeon

Believer, Jesus is the federal head of His elect. Every redeemed soul is one with the Lord from heaven since He is the Second Adam, the Sponsor and Substitute of the elect in the new covenant of love.

Thus, whatever Christ has done, He has worked for the whole body of His Church. God does not look upon her as separate from her covenant head. As the Anointed Redeemer of Israel, Christ Jesus has nothing distinct from His Church, but all that He has He holds for her.

Adam's righteousness was ours so long as he maintained it, and his sin was ours the moment that he committed it; and in the same manner, all that Jesus the Second Adam is or does is ours as well as His, seeing that He is our representative.

Here is the foundation of the covenant of grace. This gracious system of representation and substitution is the very groundwork of the gospel of our salvation, and is to be received with strong faith and rapturous joy.[52]

☙ Lesson 14 ❧

Superiority of the New Covenant

Hebrews 8:8-13

Part I: Setting the Stage

Purpose

This lesson looks at an Old Testament proof text predicting the need for a new covenant. The establishment of a new covenant to accomplish what the Mosaic Law could not accomplish was foretold by the prophet Jeremiah nearly six centuries before Christ. It is important for us to appreciate what the superior new covenant predicted by Jeremiah means for our salvation.

Look for the following application points in this lesson:

1. God enables us to obey Him through the new covenant written in our minds and hearts.
2. God forgives our sins in the new covenant mediated by Jesus Christ.
3. The new covenant is a matter of eternal life and death.

The Abrahamic Covenant

There are several important covenants mentioned in the Bible.[53] The author has already referred to God's covenant with Abraham and the covenant promises of descendants, land, and being a blessing to the world. As discussed in Lesson 10, God has sworn to fulfill the Abrahamic covenant.

The covenant promises were partially fulfilled through Abraham's physical descendants living in the land of Canaan. Longer-term messianic

136

fulfillment of the covenant promises will be accomplished by God through Abraham's descendant Jesus Christ and His church.[54]

The Mosaic Covenant

The covenant God made with Moses was established approximately five hundred years after the Abrahamic covenant. The Mosaic covenant or Mosaic Law administered the blessings of the Abrahamic covenant based on the people's obedience.

Although the Mosaic covenant was not the oldest covenant chronologically, it is called the "old covenant" or "first covenant" in contrast to the new covenant that fulfilled and replaced it.

The Mosaic covenant mediated by Moses set up the Levitical priesthood, guided national Israel, and prepared people for salvation in Jesus Christ. It was a useful covenant that served its purpose well, but it was temporary and limited. Its main faults were that it could not enable the obedience of God's people, it could not secure lasting salvation, and it could not completely cleanse people's guilty consciences.

The New Covenant

The new covenant of grace in Jesus Christ fulfilled and replaced the old Mosaic covenant of law. The new covenant administers the blessings of the Abrahamic covenant on the basis of Christ's obedience. God's people are to put their faith in Christ as their representative in covenant obedience.

Fulfillment of the new covenant began at Christ's first coming and will be completed at His second coming. The new covenant will never be replaced because God swore an oath and made Jesus the guarantor.

Replacing the old Mosaic covenant with a new one was deadly serious business. The old covenant had been in effect for 1,500 years and no person had the right to change it. Anyone accused of changing the law could face death by stoning. The gravity of the situation helps us understand why the author was careful to build his case for the new covenant on God's ancient word. The author would not want to be accused of changing the old covenant of his own accord. It was important to remind people that it was God who established the old covenant, foretold its insufficiency, and replaced it with a permanent and unbreakable new covenant.

Today the new covenant is still a matter of physical life and death for those who take the risk of proclaiming it in hostile places. It is also a matter of eternal spiritual life and death for every person. We are meant to enjoy a loving covenant relationship with God through Christ now and forever.

Part II: Studying Scripture

The author quotes Jeremiah's prophecy predicting the new covenant. This is the third Old Testament proof text in Hebrews that implies the old covenant was insufficient for fulfillment of what God offered. The three proof texts are summarized below:

The Need for the New Covenant

Eternal rest: Believers need to live in God's presence now and forever. (Hebrews 4:7-8 from Psalm 95:7-8)
Lasting salvation: Believers need a perfect high priest who lives forever. (Hebrews 7:11, 17 from Psalm 110:4)
Covenant obedience: Believers need renewed hearts and minds for obedience. (Hebrews 8:8-9 from Jeremiah 31:31-34)

Read Jeremiah 11:9-11

1. People In Need of a New Covenant

The prophet Jeremiah lived in the southern kingdom of Judah a century after the northern kingdom of Israel had been destroyed by the Assyrians. Jeremiah warned Judah that they would be destroyed like Israel if they did not turn from their idolatry and sin. Jeremiah's prophecies of doom were fulfilled when the Babylonians repeatedly invaded Judah and deported many Jews into exile in Babylon by 586 B.C.

a) In v. 10, what was Judah's sin?

b) In v. 11, how would God punish their sin?

c) The Babylonian siege of Jerusalem, Judah's capital, lasted two and a half horrific years. In the book of Lamentations, Jeremiah records suffering and death by sword, pestilence, famine, and cannibalism during the siege. Judah's ensuing exile in Babylon lasted seventy years. What does the severity of God's punishment tell us about the seriousness of breaking the covenant?

d) Read Jeremiah 29:10-13. These memorable verses come from a letter sent by Jeremiah to the exiles in Babylon. Jeremiah had been allowed by the Babylonians to stay in war-torn Judah. He wrote to the exiles to give them hope that God would one day restore them. Which part of his message would have been most encouraging to you as an exile? Which part encourages you today?

Read Jeremiah 31:31-34

2. Predicting the New Covenant

Through Jeremiah, God foretold that He would one day institute a new covenant that would empower His people for covenant obedience. This is the passage quoted in Hebrews.

a) In v. 31, God says He will make a new covenant with Israel and Judah although neither kingdom existed at that point. The wording emphasizes the unity of God's covenant people no matter how far they are scattered in space or time. Jesus instituted the new covenant with the new Israel, the true spiritual descendants of Abraham, the universal church. What steps will you take to gain a greater sense of unity with the church around the world?

b) In v. 32, what did the exiles unfortunately have in common with the Israelites in the wilderness a thousand years earlier? Note that under the old covenant the Israelites were punished with permanent exile from Canaan, but the new covenant of grace offers restoration to the exiles in Babylon.

c) In v. 32, how does Christ's relationship with the church redeem and fulfill the Old Testament image of God being the husband of unfaithful Israel (see Ephesians 5:25-27, 31-32)?

d) The old covenant was mediated by Moses after the redemption of God's people from Egypt. The new covenant was mediated by Jesus after the redemption of God's people from sin. The pattern is that God saves His people for the purpose of a covenant relationship with Him. How would you counsel a friend who wants salvation but does not want a relationship with God that involves obedience to His word?

Read Hebrews 8:8-12

3. Benefits of the New Covenant

a) In v. 10, Jeremiah says the new covenant will be instituted after "those days" or "that time," referring to a future time after the Exile. Why would the hope of a new covenant motivate God's people to keep the faith during exile?

b) The old covenant outwardly commanded people's obedience but did not provide the indwelling power of the Holy Spirit so they could obey. This power to obey is one of the key differences between the old and new covenants. On what did God write His law of the old covenant (see Exodus 31:18)? In v. 10, where does God write the new covenant?

c) In v. 12, God promises not to remember our sins. It is not that He cannot recall them, but He does not hold them against us in condemnation. This complete forgiveness is another key difference between the old and new covenants. Under the old covenant of law there were sins for which there was no sacrifice of atonement (murder, adultery, etc.). What is your response to the good news that in the new covenant repentant sinners are forgiven?

4. Summary of the New Covenant Promises

Write in your own words four important promises God makes or renews in the new covenant:

8:10 _____

_____

8:11 _____

8:12 _____

Read Hebrews 8:13

5. End of the Old Covenant

A modern analogy to the author's argument can be found when a technology company announces a new product. As soon as the advertisement comes out we know the old product is basically obsolete, even if the new one will not be available for a while. We continue to use the old product while we wait for the new one to appear.

a) In v. 13a, what did Jeremiah's prophecy of a new covenant mean for the old covenant in his day?

b) In v. 13b, what was happening to the old covenant when Hebrews was written?

c) What is the inevitable end result of growing old or aging?

d) Without the old covenant there was no basis for the Levitical priesthood, ceremonial law, Temple, altar, and other elements of sacrificial worship. These elements were fulfilled and replaced by Jesus' priesthood in the new covenant, and they vanished forever when the Romans destroyed the Temple in Jerusalem in A.D. 70.

When people today insist that the Temple and altar in Jerusalem be rebuilt for worship, they are unfortunately advocating a return to the old covenant. Why does a return to the old covenant deny the sufficiency of Christ's sacrifice and priesthood?

6. A Matter of Life and Death

You may have noticed that in every chapter of Hebrews the author quotes proof texts from the Jewish Bible, the Old Testament, to support his reasoning. He was wise to exercise caution while teaching that the old covenant had been replaced. The new covenant creates tension and hostility wherever it is boldly proclaimed.

a) Read Acts 6:13-14 and 7:58. What was the charge against Stephen with regard to the Mosaic Law? What happened to him?

b) Read Acts 21:28-33. What was the charge against Paul with regard to the Mosaic Law? What happened to him?

c) Read Matthew 10:16-22. According to this passage, what should be our attitude when we evangelize? How should we expect unbelievers to react? In v. 22, why is it important for us to persevere in faith?

Part III: Personal Application and Growth

Today's lesson points to several important truths that apply to our personal lives. Allow these truths to penetrate your mind, soften your heart, deepen your faith and affect your behavior to help you continually grow in Christ.

1. God enables us to obey Him through the new covenant written in our minds and hearts.

Because of the new covenant, the Holy Spirit indwells believers in a way that was not commonly available in Old Testament times. The Spirit brings Scripture to our mind and guides us every moment of the day, not audibly but through impressions on our mind and heart. Starting today, how will you learn to better recognize the Spirit's guidance in your life?

2. God forgives our sins in the new covenant mediated by Jesus Christ.

How will you counsel a Christian friend who is truly repentant for his or her sin, but fears it is too grievous for God to forgive?

3. The new covenant is a matter of eternal life and death.

In his final sermon, Christian apologist C. S. Lewis warns that if you haven't chosen the kingdom of God, it makes no difference in the end what you have chosen instead:

> "We shall have missed the end for which we are formed and rejected the only thing that satisfies. Does it matter to a man dying in the desert by which choice of route he missed the only well?"[55]

What will you do this week to deepen your awareness of the eternal significance of the new covenant of grace?

Part IV: Closing Devotion

by Charles Spurgeon

Believer, the Lord's people delight in the new covenant itself. It is an unfailing source of consolation to them. It is peculiarly pleasing to them to remember the *sureness* of the covenant. It often makes their hearts dilate with joy to think of its *immutability*, for it is a covenant which neither time nor eternity, life nor death, shall ever be able to violate – a covenant as everlasting as the Rock of Ages.

They rejoice also to feast upon the *fullness* of this covenant, for they see in it all things provided for them. God is their portion, Christ their companion, the Spirit their Comforter, earth their lodge, and heaven their home. Oh!, how their souls were gladdened when they saw in the last will and testament of their divine kinsman, that it was bequeathed to them!

More especially it is the pleasure of God's people to contemplate the *graciousness* of this covenant. Grace is the basis, grace the condition, grace the substance, grace the bulwark, grace the foundation, grace the topstone. The new covenant of grace is a treasury of wealth, a granary of food, a fountain of life, a store-house of salvation, a charter of peace, and a haven of joy.[56]

❧ Lesson 15 ❧

The Sanctuary on Earth

Hebrews 9:1-10

Part I: Setting the Stage

Purpose

This lesson points out that the Tabernacle was designed to teach worshipers about the holiness and nearness of God. The earthly sanctuary was a copy of the heavenly sanctuary where Jesus Christ now ministers in God's presence as our high priest. Jesus has opened the way to the heavenly holy places so we may follow Him there. It is important for us to remember that our holy God invites us to draw near to Him through Christ.

Look for the following application points in this lesson:

1. God is to be worshiped by means of the sanctuary, sacrifice, and high priest of His choosing, all of which are fulfilled in Jesus Christ.
2. The earthly Tabernacle and Temple represented both God's presence and holiness.
3. Heaven is the invisible, true sanctuary where we have access to God through Christ.

A Sanctuary of God's Choosing

God is enthroned in heaven but He desires to have fellowship with humans on earth. He is willing to make Himself known to humanity and He condescends to dwell among His people. By pure grace He invites us to enjoy a loving relationship with Him, and even though we are sinful, He provides a way for us to come into His holy and perfect presence.

Under the old covenant the Tabernacle (later the Temple) symbolized God's presence in the midst of His people. God ordained that it should be the only authorized central place of worship. The main activity of the Tabernacle was the priestly offering of sacrifices and prayers to God on behalf of the people.

Under the new covenant Jesus Christ fulfills God's requirements for worship. Jesus is the perfect high priest appearing in the perfect heavenly sanctuary on the basis of His perfect sacrifice. Christ alone makes it possible for us to come into God's holy presence.

The Tabernacle

God instructed Moses how to build the Tabernacle based on a heavenly pattern. The Tabernacle and later the Temple were temporary symbols that pointed to a heavenly reality.

The Tabernacle was a rectangular covered tent divided by a curtain into two sacred rooms that held gold furnishings. The first or outer room was the Holy Place. It contained a lampstand (*menorah*) with seven lights; a table of showbread (bread of the Presence); and an altar of incense near the curtained entrance to the Most Holy Place. The second or inner room, the Most Holy Place (Holy of Holies), contained the ark of the covenant.

The term Tabernacle sometimes also referred to the surrounding open air courtyard where the bronze altar of burnt offerings and the priests' bronze wash basin were located. People entered the curtained courtyard through the east gate with their sin offerings, and the priests entered the hidden holy places on their behalf. The materials of the Tabernacle increased in value as one moved east to west toward God's presence in the Most Holy Place.

Levitical worship provided a rich sensory experience. The sanctuary glittered with gold; the high priestly garments shone with precious jewels. The smell of oil, sacrificial blood, cooked meat, fresh bread, wine, and incense hung in the air. The sound of the *shofar* (horn) called people to worship, and age-old psalms were sung in joyful processionals toward the Temple.

It is no wonder the author of Hebrews felt the need to exhort all believers to lift their eyes off earthly things and focus on the unseen reality and riches of heaven where Christ lives and intercedes. Christians in any age can find it hard to accept the superiority of an invisible heavenly sanctuary. In this life we look to Christ in the magnificent heavenly sanctuary through eyes of faith.

Part II: Studying Scripture

Read Exodus 25:8-9, 31-40

1. The Pattern of the Tabernacle

Moses made several trips up Mount Sinai to be instructed by God about the law, the priesthood, and the construction of the Tabernacle and its furnishings. The pattern of the earthly sanctuary reflected the heavenly reality on which it was based.

a) In v. 8, what was the purpose of the earthly sanctuary?

b) In v. 9, who designed the earthly sanctuary? What was Moses' role?

c) In v. 31-40, God laid out instructions for making the lampstand (*menorah*) for the Tabernacle. Glance at other headings in chapters 25-30 to get a sense of God's detailed instructions regarding materials, value, size, location, decoration, and function of the items in the Tabernacle as well as the priestly garments. How does the attention to detail show that it matters to God how He is worshiped?

d) Read Numbers 1:51-53. The Tabernacle represented God's presence among His people. In the wilderness, the Tabernacle was located in the center of the Israelite tribes whether they were marching or camping. Who guarded the Tabernacle? Whose wrath were the people being protected from?

Read Hebrews 9:1-5

The author mentions the furnishings of the holy places in the Tabernacle as the context for discussing the priests' duties. His readers would have been well aware of the symbolism of the furnishings. Modern readers may not be as familiar with the symbolism, so we will take time to review each item. The furnishings of the holy places have been fulfilled in Jesus Christ.

2. The Holy Place

The Holy Place was where God's people, through their representative priests, drew near to His presence.

a) Read Isaiah 60:1-3. The lampstand symbolized God's chosen people, Israel. What was the source of Israel's light and what was its purpose? God's promises to Israel were inherited by the true Israel, the church, the body of Christ. Give specific examples of how the church acts as a lampstand shining the light of God's glory in the world today.

b) The table of showbread displayed the bread of the Presence, a thank offering to God consisting of twelve loaves of bread representing the twelve tribes of Israel. In what way was Jesus' sacrifice a bread offering to God on behalf of God's people (see John 6:51)?

c) The author associates the altar of incense with the Most Holy Place, possibly because the incense censer was used there on the Day of Atonement, but the altar itself was located in the Holy Place. The people's prayers were symbolically lifted to God in the smoke of sacred incense twice a day. In the new covenant, how are believers' prayers lifted up to God (see Hebrews 7:25)?

d) The three furnishings of the Holy Place reminded worshipers to maintain a proper attitude as they drew near to God through their representative priests, as summarized below.

The Holy Place

Furnishings	Worshipers' Proper Attitude
Lampstand (*menorah*)	Be a reflection of God's glory.
Table of showbread	Be continually grateful to God.
Altar of incense	Be prayerful.

Which of these attitudes should be more evident in your life? How will you develop them?

3. The Most Holy Place

The Most Holy Place was where God descended to meet with His people's representative high priest. It contained the ark of the covenant which was a chest with a lid that served as God's throne, also called the mercy seat or atonement cover. The ark was symbolically guarded by two gold cherubim with outstretched wings, and it initially held three items described below.

a) The urn of manna was a reminder of God's provision and salvation of His people in the wilderness. He met the needs of the Israelites so they could live. How does Jesus, the true manna or bread from heaven, ultimately fulfill the purpose of the wilderness manna?

b) Aaron's staff that budded was proof that God chose Aaron's line from the tribe of Levi to serve as priests. God's people were to approach Him through a representative priest. The Levitical priesthood became obsolete when Jesus Christ became high priest in the order of Melchizedek. What was the proof that God chose Jesus to replace the Levitical priesthood (Hebrews 7:28)?

c) The stone tablets contained the Ten Commandments, a summary of Mosaic Law. Why was it necessary for the old covenant mediated by Moses to be replaced and fulfilled by the new covenant mediated by Jesus (Hebrews 8:6-7)?

d) The three items in the ark of the covenant in the Most Holy Place reminded worshipers of God's loving presence and provision for His people, as summarized below.

The Most Holy Place

Items in the Ark	God's Presence and Provision
Urn of manna	God provides for His people's needs.
Aaron's staff that budded	God provides a way to be approached.
Stone tablets of law	God provides a covenant relationship.

Which of these aspects of God's presence and provision do you tend to take for granted? How will you deepen your appreciation of them?

Read Hebrews 9:6-10

4. Serving in the Earthly Tabernacle

a) In v. 6, who was allowed to enter the Holy Place and what happened there?

b) In v. 7, who was allowed to enter the Most Holy Place and what happened there?

c) What do you think the restricted access to God's holy presence was meant to teach people?

5. No Longer Valid

a) In v. 8-10, as long as the Holy Place or Tabernacle was "still standing," meaning as long as the old covenant had valid standing in God's eyes, what were the limited consequences?

b) The Tabernacle had been a valid symbol of the old covenant in its time, but was no longer valid in the re-formation or new order established by Christ's death. In the new covenant believers are forgiven and do not have to be separated from God's holy presence, nor do they need a flawed earthly priest to serve as a mediator between worshipers and God.

    Since we do not need earthly mediators, what should be the role of ordained church leaders today?

c) Give examples of the kind of leadership implied by the titles pastor (shepherd), minister (servant of the Lord), and elder. How will you support your ordained leaders' efforts to guide, care, and serve?

6. Modern Church Buildings

There is no need for a central earthly Tabernacle or Temple, for its purpose has been fulfilled by Christ in the heavenly sanctuary. However, the design of a local church sanctuary can still teach worshipers something about God.

a) How does the height and design of a sanctuary ceiling lead worshipers to ponder either God's holy transcendence (distance) or His loving immanence (nearness)? For example, consider a cathedral and a small chapel.

b) How can the chancel area at the front of a sanctuary be designed to convey the truth that access to God's presence is no longer restricted to earthly priests?

c) Why do many Protestant sanctuaries have a communion table, not an altar?

d) The pulpit may be the dominant piece of furniture in the sanctuary, often located in the center of the chancel. What does this convey about the pre-eminence of God's word?

e) What do you like about your local church sanctuary? How does its design encourage you to turn your thoughts to Jesus' high priestly ministry?

Part III: Personal Application and Growth

Today's lesson points to several important truths that apply to our personal lives. Allow these truths to penetrate your mind, soften your heart, deepen your faith and affect your behavior to help you continually grow in Christ.

1. God is to be worshiped by means of the sanctuary, sacrifice, and high priest of His choosing, all of which are fulfilled in Jesus Christ.

When you attend your church's weekly worship service, notice what each aspect of worship tells you about the priesthood of Jesus Christ. How will your worship be enriched by paying attention to these aspects?

2. The earthly Tabernacle and Temple represented both God's presence and holiness.

What do you tend to appreciate more, God's loving nearness (immanence) or His holy otherness (transcendence)? What will you do to hold both attributes in high esteem?

3. Heaven is the invisible, true sanctuary where we have access to God through Christ.

The Tabernacle's design was a reminder that God is holy, other, set apart, transcendent, perfect and majestic, but He is also accessible to sinful people through the mediator of His choosing. Theologian R. C. Sproul points out that God's provision of a mediator who accomplishes our atonement by His once-for-all sacrifice sets Christianity apart:

> "The great difference between Christianity and other world religions regarding God's holiness is found in the concept of atonement.... I don't see how the other world religions could be comfortable with the fact of human

sinfulness and the fact of the holiness of God *without* a mediator, without a Savior."[57]

What steps will you take to keep your eyes on our Mediator and Savior Jesus Christ, avoiding pressure from the world to downgrade either the seriousness of your sinful condition or the holiness of God?

Part IV: Closing Devotion
by Charles Spurgeon

Believer, the consecrated lamps in the Tabernacle could not give light without oil. Not every oil might be used in the Lord's service. Neither the petroleum which exudes so plentifully from the earth, nor the produce of fishes, nor that extracted from nuts would be accepted; one oil only was selected, and that the best olive oil (Exodus 27:20).

Our churches are the Savior's golden candelabra, and if they are to be lights in this dark world they must have much holy oil. Truth, holiness, joy, knowledge, and love are all beams of the sacred light, but we cannot give them forth unless we receive the oil of gospel grace from God the Holy Spirit.

Pretended grace from natural goodness, fancied grace from priestly hands, or imaginary grace from outward ceremonies will never serve the true saints of God; they know that the Lord would not be pleased with rivers of such oil. They go to the olive-press of Gethsemane and draw their supplies from Christ who was crushed therein. Let us pray for ourselves, our ministers, and our churches, that they may never lack oil for the light.[58]

❧ Lesson 16 ❧

The Sanctuary in Heaven

Hebrews 9:11-28

Part I: Setting the Stage

Purpose

This lesson focuses on Jesus Christ's entrance into the heavenly holy places on the basis of His atoning blood. Christ continues to minister in the heavenly sanctuary forever as our high priest. It is important for us to anchor our hope of salvation on Christ in the innermost places of heaven, in the unseen but superior sanctuary that Christ has made accessible to believers.

Look for the following application points in this lesson:

1. Jesus Christ entered the heavenly holy places on the basis of His atoning blood.
2. We enter heaven not by being good enough, but by belonging to Christ.
3. Christ opened the way into the heavenly sanctuary so we may draw near to God.

Entering Heaven

Having been reminded in the last lesson that the earthly Tabernacle was a copy of heaven, we now turn our attention to heaven itself.

The book of Hebrews does not dwell on what life will be like once we are in heaven as much as it emphasizes how to enter heaven in the first place. As our representative, Jesus entered the true sanctuary heaven on the basis of His perfect blood sacrifice. We enter heaven solely on the basis of faith in Jesus' work, not by our own good deeds or righteousness. Christ's atoning work on the cross means our sins were imputed to Him and His righteousness was imputed to us. Entering heaven is connected to the shedding of atoning blood.

The Old Covenant Needed Atoning Blood

Both the old and new covenants had to be inaugurated by atoning blood. The author presents a proof text to remind us of Moses' ratification ceremony of the old covenant at Mount Sinai. By now we should be familiar with the author's pattern of presenting Old Testament proof texts to reinforce his point.

It will be helpful for us to recall the events leading up to the sealing of the old covenant. First, through Moses God offered to have a special covenant relationship with the Israelites, and the people accepted (Exodus 19). Then God orally summarized His covenant law in the Ten Commandments followed by details of the law, and the people accepted (Exodus 20-23).

Moses wrote the law on a scroll, built an altar for animal sacrifice, and assembled the people for a ratification ceremony. He sprinkled half the sacrificial blood on the altar, representing God's acceptance of the people's offerings. Then he again read the law to the people and they once again promised to obey. Moses sprinkled the other half of the blood on the people, representing their vow to obey the covenant (Exodus 24).

The ratification ceremony was followed by a covenant meal where the elders of Israel celebrated sealing the covenant. At this point God invited Moses to come up the mountain to receive the Ten Commandments on stone tablets. Moses stayed on Mount Sinai for forty days and nights (Exodus 24-31).

The New Covenant Needed Atoning Blood

Just as the old covenant was inaugurated by sacrificial blood, so was the new covenant. In both cases God allowed the people to be represented by substitutionary blood so the people could live. Christ offered His blood of the new covenant at the cross on our behalf and entered the heavenly sanctuary on the basis of His sacrifice. His sacrifice was necessary, complete, and final.

God had prepared His people to understand Christ's offering through the Passover and Exodus out of Egypt. The angel of death passed over Hebrew homes in Egypt wherever blood of a sacrificial lamb was sprinkled on doorposts. The Passover foreshadowed the sacrifice of Christ, the Lamb of God who saves God's people by the covering of His blood.

In addition, the covenant meal after ratification of the old covenant foreshadowed the Last Supper where Christ and His apostles celebrated the new covenant soon to be sealed by His death (I Corinthians 11:25-26). What an encouragement that God prepared His people to understand the truth that faith in Christ's atoning blood is the only way of salvation and the only way to heaven.

Part II: Studying Scripture

Read Hebrews 9:11-14

1. Entering the Heavenly Holy Places

Christ entered the holy places through the "tent [tabernacle] not made with hands." Various interpretations have been suggested for this tent, but it is likely that the tent refers to heaven (Hebrews 4:14; 8:2, 5). Christ went into the holy places by entering through the tent of heaven, just as the Levitical high priest went into the holy places by entering through the tent on earth.

a) In v. 11, how is the heavenly tent superior to the earthly one?

b) In v. 12, unlike a Levitical high priest entering the earthly holy places, how often did Christ enter the heavenly holy places? On the basis of what sacrifice did He enter? What did He secure or obtain for us?

c) Read Mark 15:37-38. What is the evidence that our high priest Jesus fulfilled the old covenant when He died, figuratively entering the Most Holy Place in the earthly Temple? What does it mean for you that the barrier to God's presence in the Most Holy Place was opened by Christ?

2. Purification Under the Old Covenant

a) Read Leviticus 16:11, 15-16. On the annual Day of Atonement the high priest entered the Most Holy Place. In v. 11, who did he atone for with the blood of a bull? In v. 15, who did he atone for with a goat's blood? In v. 16, why did the earthly sanctuary need atoning blood?

b) Read Numbers 19:9, 16-18. The ashes of a heifer were mixed with water to ceremonially purify anyone associated with touching a corpse. In v. 18, what else needed to be purified?

c) Read Luke 11:39. Ceremonially unclean persons under the old covenant were purified by the sprinkling of sacrificial blood or ashes. According to Jesus, why was such external ritual purification incomplete? In other words, what still remained inside the sinner?

3. Purification Under the New Covenant

The offering of Christ's blood took place on the cross. Christ entered heaven on the basis of His blood sacrifice, but He did not literally take His spilled blood into heaven the way the Levitical high priest took the sacrificial blood into the Most Holy Place.

a) In v. 13-14, the author argues from the lesser to the greater. If old covenant animal sacrifices purified a believer *externally*, then the Messiah's blood would bring even greater cleansing *internally* in the new covenant. This internal cleansing is a key difference between the old and new covenants. In v. 14b, what internal cleansing do we need?

b) In v. 14b, the phrase "dead works" may mean works that are useless for earning salvation, but probably instead refers to sinful deeds that deserve death. Under the old covenant there was no sacrifice to cover intentional sins that were subject to capital punishment. What were some categories of intentional sin (see Exodus 21:12; Leviticus 20:2, 10; 24:16)?

c) Under the new covenant, intentional sin is forgiven when there is true repentance. The new covenant can therefore cleanse one's conscience in a way the old covenant could not. At the end of v. 14b, what is Christ's ultimate purpose in securing our forgiveness?

d) The Reformer Martin Luther lamented the fact he could never punish himself enough to be purified for God, but his misery turned to joy when he realized that a cleansed conscience is attained by grace through faith in Christ:

> "Faith is a living, unshakeable confidence in God's grace... Trust in and knowledge of God's grace makes a person joyful, confident, and happy with regard to God and all creatures... A person will do good to everyone without coercion, willingly and happily; he will serve everyone, suffer everything for the love and praise of God, who has shown him such grace."[59]

How will you express your joy, confidence and happiness at being saved?

Read Hebrews 9:15-22

4. Blood of the Covenant

The Greek word for covenant is *diatheke* (DEE-uh-TAY-kay) and it has different meanings depending on its context. *Diatheke* can be translated into English as "covenant," "will," and "testament." In this passage the author seems to combine these meanings to explain that the atoning blood of Jesus was absolutely necessary to inaugurate the new covenant. The chart below summarizes the meanings.

Meanings of *Diatheke*

Covenant: A binding agreement between two living parties. A covenant was ratified by sacrificial blood signifying that if the covenant was broken, the offending party must die. The idea of covenant is used in a religious sense in Hebrews.

Will or Testament: A document by one party designating property inheritance. A will goes into effect only upon the death of the testator. The idea of a will carries a legal meaning.

---

a) In v. 15, *diatheke* means a covenant agreement. God's people sinned and broke the first covenant, forfeiting their inherited blessings. However, Christ paid the death penalty for sin and set all believers free to inherit the blessings of the new covenant. What words would you use to describe the freedom you feel due to Christ's payment?

b) In v. 16-17, *diatheke* is used in the sense of a last will and testament. Christ was God's mediator in carrying out His will and testament. Why was Christ's death necessary so that we might inherit God's blessings in the new covenant?

c) In v. 18-20, *diatheke* again has the meaning of a covenant agreement. The episode in view is Moses' ratification of the old covenant by the sprinkling of blood (Exodus 24:8). The author uses this proof text to illustrate the need for the blood of the covenant. Jesus deliberately used similar words to institute the new covenant at the Last Supper (Matthew 26:28). Why would Jesus echo the words of Moses, mediator of the old covenant?

d) In v. 21, the episode in view is Moses' consecration of the Tabernacle. The author says Moses sprinkled the tent and its furnishings with blood. How is this different from Moses' account in Leviticus 8:10? We do not know what source the author of Hebrews relied on for his account; it is possible the two accounts are describing different moments of the same event.

e) In v. 22, by what means was almost everything purified under the old covenant? How are our consciences purified and forgiven under the new covenant? The fundamental principle at work here is that blood is necessary for forgiveness because blood represents life (Leviticus 17:11). Our lives belong to God and He requires the forfeiture of our lives, or a suitable substitute of His choice, as the penalty for our sin.

Read Hebrews 9:23-28

5. The Superior Heavenly Sanctuary

a) Author and pastor Randy Alcorn suggests that God patterned earth in the image of heaven, and he cautions us not to get it backwards:

> "The book of Hebrews seems to say that we should see Earth as a *derivative* realm and Heaven as the *source* realm...Often our thinking is backwards... We tend to

start with Earth and reason up toward Heaven, when instead we should start with Heaven and reason down toward Earth."[60]

In v. 24, how does the author of Hebrews describe the relationship between the earthly Tabernacle and heaven?

b) The heavenly sanctuary did not have to be purified from sin. Rather, Christ's sacrifice purifies God's people so they will not defile the heavenly sanctuary. In v. 23-24, why did Christ appear in the heavenly sanctuary?

c) In v. 25-26, even if Jesus could repeat His death, why would our salvation be incomplete if He endlessly re-sacrificed Himself instead of endlessly serving in heaven as high priest?

6. Looking Forward to Heaven

a) In v. 27a, what normally happens at the end of life? The only exceptions in Scripture are Enoch and Elijah who were taken to heaven.

b) How does v. 27a negate the possibility of reincarnation, the idea of returning after death to live and die in a different earthly body?

c) Unbelievers often insist there is no life after death, but Scripture teaches otherwise. In v. 27b, why is there no possibility of annihilation, extinction, or nothingness after death?

d) Read Matthew 25:41, 46. What is the result of judgment? What should you be doing to take Scripture's warnings about judgment more seriously?

e) When Christ comes a second time it will not be to repeat His sacrifice. He has dealt with sin once and for all. In v. 28, what will be Christ's glorious purpose in coming at the end times? How do these closing words of the chapter offer hope to discouraged believers?

Part III: Personal Application and Growth

Today's lesson points to several important truths that apply to our personal lives. Allow these truths to penetrate your mind, soften your heart, deepen your faith and affect your behavior to help you continually grow in Christ.

1. Jesus Christ entered the heavenly holy places on the basis of His atoning blood.

Each day this week ponder the necessity of Jesus' atoning blood that secures our inheritance, redemption, forgiveness, and purification. How do you expect to see your attitude about yourself and others improve as you gain deeper humility with regard to these benefits?

2. We enter heaven not by being good enough, but by belonging to Christ.

It has been estimated that approximately 250,000 people die every day and go straight to heaven or hell. That means in the past hour over 10,400 people ran out of time to give further consideration to Jesus Christ. Take the opportunity this week to ask people if they believe they will go to heaven when they die, and why? Talk to them about the need to rely only on Christ's righteousness.

3. Christ opened the way into the heavenly sanctuary so we may draw near to God.

What will you do to ensure that your life better reflects the truth that you live in nearness to God? For example, what practical steps will you take to be more kind and patient with others when you are under stress?

Part IV: Closing Devotion
by Charles Spurgeon

Believer, Jesus is the great I AM, the entrance into the true church, and the way of access to God Himself. He gives to those who come to God by Him certain choice privileges.

They shall be saved. Entrance through Jesus into peace is the guarantee of entrance by the same door into heaven. Jesus is the only door, an open door, a wide door, a safe door; and blessed are those who rest all their hope of admission to glory upon the crucified Redeemer.

They shall go in. They shall be privileged to go in among the divine family, participating in all the honors, enjoyments, banquets of love, treasures of the covenant, and storehouses of the promises. They shall go in to the King of kings in the power of the Holy Spirit.

They shall go out. They go out into the world to labor and suffer, but what a mercy to go in the name and power of Jesus! We are called to bear witness to the truth, to cheer the disconsolate, to warn the careless, and to glorify God as His messengers, in His name and strength.[61]

❧ Lesson 17 ❦

Christ's Superior Sacrifice

Hebrews 10:1-18

Part I: Setting the Stage

Purpose

This lesson goes into more depth with regard to Christ's perfect and complete sacrifice. It is important for us to realize that the basis for God's forgiveness of our sins is Jesus Christ's atoning blood which was shed as a substitution for our own lives.

Look for the following application points in this lesson:

1. Jesus Christ's sacrifice was necessary, perfect, complete, and final.
2. Due to Christ's sacrifice we are forgiven of our sins and justified with God.
3. The Holy Spirit applies redemption to us so that we grow in sanctification.

The Sacredness of Life

All life belongs to God and is therefore to be considered sacred. The life of a creature is in its blood, so blood is also sacred. Because our lives are sacred and belong to God, any sin in our lives is a serious offense against God. God requires the forfeiture of life (the shedding of blood) as the penalty for sin.

It was purely by grace that from the beginning when sin first entered the world God allowed certain animals to be sacrificed instead of humans in order to pay the penalty to appease God's wrath. To begin with, God covered Adam and Eve's sin by shedding the blood of an animal (Genesis 3:21).

The sanctity of life and blood was reinforced in Israel with regulations such as the prohibition against eating blood, the need to purify oneself after touching blood, and the commandment not to commit murder. God ordained the Levitical sacrificial system as the means of offering substitutionary blood sacrifices so that God's people could live in peace with Him:

> "For the life of the flesh is in the blood, and I have given
> it for you on the altar to make atonement for your souls,
> for it is the blood that makes atonement by the life."
> (Leviticus 17:11)

Levitical Sacrificial Worship
The Levitical worship system in Israel brought a regulated, ongoing schedule of animal sacrifices carried out by a vast workforce. In the earliest days of the wilderness journey there were already 8,580 Levite males between thirty and fifty years old qualified to serve as priests and assistants at the Tabernacle.

The result over the years was the shedding of an immense amount of sacrificial blood. For instance, King Solomon was known to offer a thousand burnt offerings when he worshiped. It is staggering to fathom the hundreds of millions of gallons of sacrificial blood that were shed during 1,500 years of Levitical worship. Theologian Simon Kistemaker says,

> "Literally rivers of animal blood flowed because of these
> continual sacrifices; and the succession of priests, who
> served by division and were chosen by lot, seemed to be
> unending."[62]

An End to All That Blood
It must have been unbelievable to those who first heard the gospel to think that Jesus Christ accomplished the complete forgiveness of sins in His one-time sacrifice. His shed blood of the new covenant put an end to all that blood of old covenant sacrifices. It is just as astounding to believers today to think that Jesus obtained the forgiveness of their sins by shedding His blood two thousand years ago. Christ's blood is sufficient to cover all sins committed in the past, present and future.

The shed blood of Jesus secures the *justification* of believers, a term that has the judicial meaning of not guilty. It is God's one-time declaration at conversion that a believer has been made right with Him forever. As a result, God looks on the believer from that point forward "just as if" he or she had never sinned.

In addition, Jesus' blood makes possible the process of *sanctification*, a believer's life-long journey of becoming holy with the help of the Holy Spirit. The process of sanctification begins at conversion. Believers will only become entirely sanctified, perfected, and glorified after death, not in this lifetime.

The power of Jesus' blood is beyond our comprehension. All we can do is humbly place our trust in the mystery of Christ's atoning work because we cannot completely explain it and we cannot add anything to it. What an encouragement to know His atoning work of sacrifice is finished.

Part II: Studying Scripture

Read Hebrews 10:1-4

1. Repeated Levitical Sacrifices

a) In v. 1, what did the repeated Levitical sacrifices fail to do? Why?

b) In v. 2, what else did the repeated sacrifices fail to do?

c) In v. 3, what effect did the repetition of sacrifices have? Who do you think was reminded of the sins? How is this different from the new covenant (Hebrews 8:12)?

d) In v. 4, why were the old covenant animal sacrifices inadequate?

Read Hebrews 10:5-10

2. Something Better

a) The author of Hebrews quotes Psalm 40:6-8 (Septuagint version) written by David a thousand years earlier. This proof text foretells that the old sacrificial system would be replaced with the Messiah's sacrifice. In v. 5, who ultimately spoke Psalm 40? Why is it important for us to know who the real author of Biblical prophecy is?

b) You might wonder in what sense God has "not desired" sacrifices and offerings. After all, God is the one who ordained the Levitical system. Read Psalm 51:16-17 and Isaiah 1:12-17. What was wrong with the people's hearts and lives when they brought offerings? What does God really want?

c) In v. 5, what was God's plan to fulfill and replace the Levitical animal sacrifices and offerings?

d) In v. 5-6 and 8, what four categories sum up the Levitical sacrificial system, implying that God planned to replace the whole system?

3.   Christ's One-Time Sacrifice

a)   In v. 7, what did Christ come to do? What phrase tells us the whole Old Testament foretold God's will, His plan to sacrifice Christ?

b)   In v. 9, what sacrifices does "first" refer to? What is the "second" sacrifice that would fulfill and replace the first?

c)   In v. 10, why did God's will, His plan to sacrifice Christ, bring the Levitical sacrificial system to an end?

d)   Why would it be pointless to offer repeated animal sacrifices after Christ's death?

e)   The fact that we have "been sanctified" or "made holy" refers here to our new permanent status in Christ. It is along the lines of justification, a one-time change in our standing when we are united to Christ. In v. 10, how does Christ accomplish this change for us?

f)   How would you respond to a friend who claims to have been made right with God by self-focused meditation or any other way apart from Christ?

Read Hebrews 10:11-14

4. Christ's Sacrifice Accepted

Levitical priests remained standing while they performed their unending duties, but Christ our high priest is seated at God's right hand. Christ's sacrificial work is finished and accepted; now He continually intercedes for believers on its basis. Theologian F. F. Bruce explains,

> "A seated priest is the guarantee of a finished work and an accepted sacrifice. The heavenly high priest has indeed a continual ministry to discharge on his people's behalf at the Father's right hand; but that is the ministry of intercession on the basis of the sacrifice presented and accepted once for all; it is not the constant or repeated offering of his sacrifice."[63]

a) In v. 12-14, what phrases refute the idea that Christ's sacrifice can be continued, renewed, or repeated in any sense?[64] How do repeated sacrifices deny the effectiveness of Christ's sacrifice and its acceptance by God?

b) In v. 13, the author alludes to Psalm 110:1, already quoted as a proof text (Hebrews 1:13). God will see to it that the enthroned Christ is victorious over His enemies. Since Christ was enthroned as the reward for His completed work on the cross, why does His enthronement prove there is no need for another sacrifice?

c) In v. 14, Christ has "perfected" believers. The word perfect here does not mean we are morally perfect or completely holy like Him. Instead it has the meaning of justification, the permanent new status believers acquire forever when they are joined to Christ by faith. What did it take for Christ to accomplish our justified status?

d) In v. 14, the author goes on to speak of those who are "being sanctified" or "being made holy." The idea here is the process of sanctification, a life-long journey of growing in holiness. Who helps us grow in sanctification by applying to us the redemption accomplished by Christ (see II Thessalonians 2:13)?

e) In v. 10, 12 and 14, what does the author say three times about the frequency of Christ's offering? How does the frequency of Christ's offering differ from the repetition of Levitical sacrifices?

Read Hebrews 10:15-18

5. Redemption Accomplished and Applied

Christ became mediator of the new covenant after His death on the cross. The author brings up the new covenant by quoting the prophet Jeremiah, already cited (Hebrews 8:8-12). However, this time he only quotes the first and last verses of the portion pertaining to the new covenant (Jeremiah 31:33-34). These verses emphasize our justification and sanctification.

a) The author said earlier that the new covenant was foretold by God through Jeremiah's prophecy. Now in v. 15, who also bears witness to the new covenant?

b) Christ's sacrifice enables believers to grow in sanctification or holiness. In v. 16, why is it possible for believers to obey God in the new covenant? (Note that the Holy Spirit indwells believers in the new covenant in a way not normally available to believers under the old covenant.)

c) Christ's sacrifice also results in the believers' new status of justification. In v. 17, why are believers free from guilt before God in the new covenant? (Note that complete justification and forgiveness were not normally available to believers under the old covenant.)

6. Full Assurance

a) In v. 18, since God has forgiven our sins in the new covenant, what is no longer needed or possible?

b) The evangelist Francis Schaeffer advises that we can have real assurance of forgiveness because the basis of our forgiveness is the fact of the finished work of Christ in history. This is cause for gratitude:

> "If we have sinned, it is wonderful consciously to say, 'Thank you for a completed work,' after we have brought that specific sin under the finished work of Christ. While not absolutely necessary for restoration, the conscious giving of thanks brings assurance and peace."[65]

Why do you suppose our giving sincere thanks makes forgiveness more real to us?

Part III: Personal Application and Growth

Today's lesson points to several important truths that apply to our personal lives. Allow these truths to penetrate your mind, soften your heart, deepen your faith and affect your behavior to help you continually grow in Christ.

1. Jesus Christ's sacrifice was necessary, perfect, complete, and final.

How has this lesson helped you appreciate Christ's sacrifice more than you did before? How will your deepened appreciation encourage you to keep the faith?

2. Due to Christ's sacrifice we are forgiven of our sins and justified with God.

Set your clock alarm for the same time each day this week to remind you to thank the Lord for justifying you once and for all in Christ. What will you do to continue this daily habit of giving thanks?

3. The Holy Spirit applies redemption to us so that we grow in sanctification.

Growing in sanctification means we will inevitably produce evidence of the fruit of the Spirit: love, joy, peace, patience, kindness, goodness, faithfulness, gentleness, and self-control (Galatians 5:22-23). What is one practical way you will cooperate with the Spirit's sanctifying work in you so that His fruit becomes more evident in your life?

Part IV: Closing Devotion
by Charles Spurgeon

Believer, blessed be Jesus' name; there was no cause of death in Him. Neither original nor actual sin had defiled Him and He had done no man wrong. Lo, justice was offended by us, but found its satisfaction in Him.

Rivers of tears, mountains of offerings, seas of the blood of bulls, and hills of frankincense could not have availed for the removal of sin; but Jesus was cut off for us, and the cause of God's wrath was cut off at once, for sin was put away forever.

Herein is *wisdom*, whereby substitution, the sure way of atonement, was devised! Herein is *condescension*, which brought Messiah, the Prince, to wear a crown of thorns and die upon the cross! Herein is *love*, which led the Redeemer to lay down His life for His enemies!

It is not enough, however, to admire the spectacle of the innocent bleeding for the guilty; we must make sure of our share therein. The special object of the Messiah's death was the salvation of His church; have we a place among those for whom He gave His life a ransom? Upon all who believe the Lord Jesus, the blood of reconciliation has been sprinkled.

Let all who trust in the merit of Messiah's death be joyful at every remembrance of Him, and let their holy gratitude lead them to the fullest consecration to His cause.[66]

❧ Lesson 18 ❦

Benefits of Christ's Sacrifice

Hebrews 10:19-39

Part I: Setting the Stage

Purpose

This lesson points out some of the benefits we enjoy as a result of Christ's superior sacrifice. It is particularly important for us to remember that as a result of Christ's sacrifice we can approach God with confidence, knowing we are free from His condemnation of sin.

Look for the following application points in this lesson:

1. Christ's sacrifice makes it possible for us to draw near to God with confidence.
2. We are to persevere in faith to the end of life.
3. Believers should encourage one another to keep the faith.

Christ's Priesthood

The focus in Hebrews 8-10 has been on three inter-related aspects of Christ's superior priesthood: the new covenant, sanctuary, and sacrifice. As we have seen, the author supported his discussion of these aspects with Old Testament proof texts summarized in the chart below.

Christ's Superior Priesthood

New covenant: Believers are renewed and empowered to obey God.
(Hebrews 8:8-12 from Jeremiah 31)
Sanctuary: Jesus ministers forever in heaven, the perfect sanctuary.
(Hebrews 9:1-5 based on Exodus 25-30)
Sacrifice: We are at peace with God due to Jesus' atoning sacrifice.
(Hebrews 10:5-7 from Psalm 40:6-8)

Taken together, these proof texts represent the testimony of the whole Old Testament. Exodus is part of the Law; Psalms is from the Writings; and Jeremiah is from the Prophets. The point is that all of Scripture anticipated Christ's superior priesthood, including the new covenant, the heavenly sanctuary, and Jesus' sacrifice. God ordained it long ago.

Practical Benefits

The author now turns his attention to applying the doctrine of Christ to our personal lives, an emphasis that will continue for the rest of the book of Hebrews. Theological doctrine and practical living are inter-connected. Doctrine is useless unless it is lived out in tangible ways, and the way we live is based on the doctrines we believe.

Unfortunately, the importance of theological doctrine is often downplayed in churches today. Worshipers should understand that every church holds some kind of doctrinal beliefs whether they acknowledge them or not. For example, the simple statement that Jesus Christ is Lord and Savior involves a number of doctrines about Christ, God's sovereignty, salvation, covenant, and more.

The author reminds us there are many practical benefits that accompany life in Christ. Some of these benefits include the blessings of confident faith, participation in the church, endurance in faith, perseverance to the end, and no fear of condemnation.

Freedom from Fear

When the author speaks of freedom from fear of God's condemnation, he strikes a chord with those who have dealt with the criminal justice system. For example, over the years prison ministry leader Mark Casson has developed a great understanding of grace and justice. He is aware of what it means for someone to be condemned to life in prison. Parole is not always an option and there is no assurance that those who are condemned will ever be set free.

Casson sees imprisonment as an analogy for the fearful predicament humanity finds itself in. Due to our fallen spiritual condition all of us are on death row and we are helpless to do anything about it. It is only because Jesus Christ was executed in our place that our cell door is opened and we are set free by grace.[67] Christ makes it possible for us to live without fear of God's condemnation.

Part II: Studying Scripture

Read Hebrews 10:19-25

1. Confident Faith

We enter the heavenly holy places only by the blood of Jesus. Jesus opened a new (literally, "just slaughtered") and living way through the curtain or veil, that is, "through His flesh" or torn body (v. 19-20). The phrase brings to mind the curtain in the earthly Tabernacle that separated worshipers from God's presence in the Most Holy Place. Upon Jesus' death the curtain was torn, symbolizing that the way into God's presence was open (Matthew 27:50-51).

a) In v. 21, why can we approach God with confidence?

b) In v. 22, what has Christ's sacrifice accomplished for us?

c) In v. 23, we are to hold fast to "the confession of our hope." This phrase refers to the vows made at the time of our baptism and entrance into the church body. Why should we confidently hold fast to those vows without wavering? If you are not sure of the vows taken at your baptism, ask your pastor about the ones currently used in your church.

d) Write out v. 22-23. This is a good memory passage you might try to learn this week.

2. Participation in the Body

a) Believers are to look forward to the day of Christ's return. In v. 24-25, what are a few practical ways believers should support each other in keeping the faith as members of Christ's body, until Christ comes again? Which of these ways will you try to put more fully into practice?

b) Some people nickname Hebrews 10 "The Salad Chapter" because there is so much "lettuce." In v. 22-25, what does each "let us" phrase exhort believers to do? Allow this chapter's nickname to help you remember the main points of faith, hope and love mentioned in this passage.

c) Theologian Simon Kistemaker says,

> "One of the first indications of a lack of love toward God and the neighbor is for a Christian to stay away from the worship services. He forsakes the communal obligations of attending these meetings and displays the symptoms of selfishness and self-centeredness... All the members of the church have the communal task of encouraging one

another daily. Together we bear the responsibility, for we are the body of Christ."[68]

What is your reaction to the above quote? Why does it show a lack of love to other Christians and God if you stay away from worship services without good cause? In what ways would you be depriving the body of Christ?

d) Give an example of a time when it encouraged your faith to see someone exert unusual personal effort to regularly attend worship services. Why did you find it encouraging?

e) How would you explain to a Christian friend who often neglects worship services why you think it honors your friend, other believers, and Christ to be present at church?

Read Hebrews 10:26-31

3. No Fear of Condemnation

Now we come to a warning reminiscent of chapter 6. People who persist in ongoing sin despite knowledge of Christ show that they have rejected Him and His way of salvation. The author pointed out in Hebrews 6:4-8 that apart from Christ there is no sacrifice for sins and no possibility of forgiveness. The consequence for those who are condemned is fearful.

a) In v. 26-27, what is the fate of those who keep sinning despite knowing the truth of Christ? This is not a popular message in today's culture. Based on these verses, how would you confirm to an acquaintance that only believers are free from the fear of God's condemnation?

b) In v. 28-29, in an argument from the lesser to the greater, the author says that unbelievers among God's people who rejected the old Mosaic covenant deserved death; therefore, those who reject the superior new covenant in Christ deserve much worse punishment.[69] In v. 29, when one rejects the new covenant, what offenses are committed against the following:

The person of Christ: _____
The work of Christ: _____
The Holy Spirit: _____

c) In v. 30, the author quotes two proof texts from the Song of Moses (Deuteronomy 32:35-36). Moses brought the children of the rebellious Israelites to the edge of the Promised Land and recorded for future generations the goodness and saving work of the LORD, and the calamity that awaits those who deliberately reject His salvation.[70] How does it make you feel to know that ultimately God will deal out justice and vengeance?

d) In v. 31, what does the author of Hebrews say about *unbelievers* falling into the hands of the living God?

e) Read II Samuel 24:14. David faced God's punishment for taking an unauthorized census. What does David say *believers* can expect when they fall into the hands of the living God?

Read Hebrews 10:32-39

4. Past Endurance

a) As usual, the author encourages his readers after admonishing them. He reminds them of their past faithfulness so they will continue to persevere. In v. 32-34, what kinds of sufferings have the readers experienced?

b) In v. 34a, it was essential for the church to show practical compassion to Christians imprisoned for their faith. Jails did not provide food, blankets, or medicine, and a prisoner was dependent on loved ones for care. Why might it have been risky to provide for and associate with imprisoned Christians?

c) In v. 34b, when the readers lost property due to persecution, what was their attitude even though they were new in the faith? What do you think is their better and abiding possession?

d) What first-hand experience have you had with suffering for Christ's sake? Why do you think the average Christian in our country has not suffered more?

5.   Present Endurance

a) In v. 35, why should the readers not throw away their confidence?

b) The idea of throwing away implies that believers have some control over the matter. Why do we have to be purposeful about keeping confident faith? What challenges could weaken our faith? How will you guard against them?

c) In v. 36, believers who do the will of God will receive the promises of salvation. How does a believer know what is the overall will of God (see Hebrews 8:10)? How should this knowledge of the will of God guide you in everyday situations?

6. Perseverance to the End

In order to encourage his readers to persevere in faith to the end of life, the author quotes two prophets who understood adversity, Haggai and Habakkuk.

a) In v. 37, the third proof text says the Lord has promised to come in "a little while" (Haggai 2:6). This reference to the end times reassures us that God is in control and suffering will not last forever. What do you find comforting in this promise?

b) In v. 37, the fourth proof text assures us that God's Messiah will not delay in coming to save His people. "For still the vision awaits its appointed time... if it seems slow, wait for it; it will surely come; it will not delay" (Habakkuk 2:3). In our day it has been over two thousand years since Christ's first coming, but there has been no delay in His return.

How do you feel knowing God's plan of salvation is being worked out according to His mysterious but perfect time schedule?

c) In v. 38, the author quotes a fifth proof text to affirm that God's righteous people will "live by faith" (Habakkuk 2:4).[71] What does it look like for you to live by faith in spite of the adversity you currently face in your life?

d) In v. 39, what will happen to unbelievers who fall away under persecution? What will happen to believers who persevere in faith? Why will it be easier to persevere if we strengthen our faith before persecution occurs?

Part III: Personal Application and Growth

Today's lesson points to several important truths that apply to our personal lives. Allow these truths to penetrate your mind, soften your heart, deepen your faith and affect your behavior to help you continually grow in Christ.

1. Christ's sacrifice makes it possible for us to draw near to God with confidence.

No one understands exactly how Christ's sacrifice accomplishes the removal of sin (expiation) and appeasement of God's wrath (propitiation). Christ's atoning work is real but something of a mystery. Despite the mystery, how will you demonstrate full assurance in Christ's work?

2. We are to persevere in faith to the end of life.

Starting this week, which spiritual habits will you strive to develop more fully in order to maintain confident faith? Take into consideration the areas of prayer, Bible study, corporate worship, private devotions, mercy ministry, evangelism, personal morality, and financial stewardship.

3. Believers should encourage one another to keep the faith.

What steps will you take to arrange your schedule to ensure your weekly presence at worship services? How will you become more closely connected with others in your local church in addition to attending worship services, in order to encourage them to keep the faith?

Part IV: Closing Devotion

by Charles Spurgeon

Believer, when Jesus gave Himself for us, He gave us all the rights and privileges which went with Himself; so that now, although as eternal God He has essential rights to which no creature may venture to pretend, yet as Jesus the Mediator, the federal Head of the covenant of grace, He has no heritage apart from us. All the glorious consequences of His obedience unto death are the joint riches of all who are in Him.

He enters into glory, but not for Himself alone. He appears in the presence of God for us. Consider this, believer. You have no right to heaven in yourself; your right lies in Christ:

> If you are *pardoned*, it is through His blood;
> If you have been *justified*, it is through His righteousness;
> If you are being *sanctified*, it is because He has made possible your sanctification;
> If you will be *perfected* at the last, it will be because you are complete in Him.

Thus, Jesus is magnified, for all is in Him and by Him. The inheritance is made certain to us, for it is obtained in Him. Each blessing is the sweeter, and even heaven itself the brighter, because it is Jesus our Beloved in whom we have obtained all.[72]

SECTION IV

PRACTICAL EVIDENCE

OF OUR SALVATION

❧ Lesson 19 ❦

Confident Faith

Hebrews 11:1-22

Part I: Setting the Stage

Purpose

This lesson honors God's faithful Old Testament heroes, particularly the patriarchs, for they believed God's promises of salvation without seeing fulfillment. Believers today have the advantage of knowing Jesus Christ as Savior, but along with the people of old we have not seen Him in person. We must take it on faith that Christ lives and intercedes for us in heaven. It is important for us to strengthen our faith by imitating believers who demonstrated confident faith in God's unseen saving work.

Look for the following application points in this lesson:

1. Faith is the assurance of things hoped for, the conviction of things not seen.
2. We should imitate the confident faith of past believers.
3. The patriarchs believed God without seeing fulfillment in their lifetimes.

Remembering the Big Picture

Up to this point the author has presented foundational doctrines about Jesus Christ in order to ground our faith in who Jesus is and what He has done. The author has also reminded us that theological doctrines are to be lived out in practical ways. Throughout the remainder of Hebrews he exhorts us to imitate the faith of past believers, maintain hope in what Christ is doing in heaven, and show brotherly love to one another.

The following brief summary shows the progression of topics in Hebrews:

Main Topics in Hebrews

	Chapter
The Person of Jesus Christ	1-2
(His divine and human natures in one person)	
The Work of Jesus Christ	3-10
(His messianic fulfillment of prophet, priest and king)	
Personal Application	11-13
(Our daily practice of faith, hope and brotherly love)	

Heroes of the Faith

The list of historical heroes in Hebrews 11 has made this a favorite chapter for generations of believers. The Old Testament heroes trusted God, although often imperfectly.

The author refers to about sixteen characters by name plus countless unnamed others. Not everything in the lives of these heroes is worthy of imitation, but at some point each person demonstrated faith in God's saving promises without the benefit of seeing complete fulfillment in their lifetime. They all died before Jesus Christ came into the world.

It is their faith in the unseen things of God that we are to imitate: faith in His existence, His character, and His words and saving actions. We are all called to live faithfully to the best of our ability, in whatever generation and circumstances God has ordained.

The First Major Group: Confident Heroes

The heroes of Hebrews 11 can be grouped into two major time periods. This lesson will focus on the first period covering the time from Creation to the patriarchs. See the Endnotes for specific Scripture references pertaining to the heroes of the faith in this lesson.[73] The next lesson will study the second major period from Moses to the prophets.

In the time from Creation to the Flood, Abel, Enoch and Noah were righteous men known for their confident faith in God despite living among unbelievers. Around 2000 B.C. Abraham (Abram) was called by God to establish a covenant people set apart for God. The patriarchs Abraham, Isaac, Jacob and Joseph were confident that God would keep His covenant promises of land and descendants and would bless the world through His elect people.

We all need heroes to imitate. We need men and women who demonstrate godly values and morals, confidence in God, courage in the face of danger and difficulty, and enduring faith. The Bible provides us with such heroes, and when we read their stories and identify with their faith we can be encouraged to persevere despite the challenges we face today.

Part II: Studying Scripture

The author begins with faith in the Creator. He takes for granted the Biblical view that God is the eternal, uncreated, personal Spirit who made all physical matter. This creationist view is commonly opposed today by a materialist view that says physical matter is the eternal, uncreated, impersonal, and sole reality from which the universe evolved. Both views must be taken on faith since no human was present at Creation and neither view can be proved scientifically.

Read Hebrews 11:1-3

1. In the Beginning

a) Faith is concerned with things hoped for. This is not wishful thinking, but certainty of what is not visible. In v. 1, how is this confident faith in the unseen things of God described?

b) The creationist view teaches that God has revealed in general terms how the universe came into being. In v. 3, how did God create the universe? (See also Genesis 1:6-10; Psalm 33:6, 9.)

c) In v. 3, the universe ("what is seen") was not formed from any pre-existing matter. Physical matter did not exist until God created it out of nothing (*ex nihilo*) by His word. When you ponder this aspect of the Creation, what words describe your reaction?

d) The materialist view described in this lesson is a man-made philosophy asserting that physical matter is the only reality. It denies the reality of a metaphysical being such as God. Why is it impossible to know the true origin of the universe while holding this view?

e) Materialists have faith in man-made hypotheses about the origin of the universe, while creationists have faith in God's account in Scripture. Why is it appropriate for creationists to assert, with a gentle attitude of course, that their truth claims are valid and even superior?

Read Hebrews 11:4-7

2. Before Abraham

a) Abel, the eldest son of Adam and Eve, was commended by God for bringing a more acceptable sacrifice than his brother Cain. Cain's basic offense was a lack of faith as seen in his failure to offer God the best of his crops. Some commentators suggest he should also have offered a blood sacrifice. Abel, on the other hand, worshiped God with a right attitude. How does your own attitude toward worship compare with Abel's?

b) Enoch was Noah's great-grandfather. Enoch walked with God and was a righteous man, as confirmed by his being taken to heaven without dying. The author of Hebrews says Enoch was commended for pleasing God. In v. 6, what must someone believe about the unseen God if he or she, like Enoch, is to draw near to God? How will this verse serve as an encouragement to you?

c) Noah obeyed God's warning to build an ark to save his family from a disastrous flood that was foretold but not yet seen. What unseen future event should motivate you to pray for the spiritual saving of loved ones while there is time (Hebrews 10:27)?

Read Hebrews 11:8-16

3. Abraham and the Promised Land

a) Around 2000 B.C. God called Abraham (Abram) to establish a covenant people for God. This was a turning point in the history of God's redemptive dealings with humanity. What does God say about the following central provisions of His covenant with Abraham?

Land (11:9) _____

Descendants (11:12) _____

b) Abraham obediently responded to God's call to leave Ur in Babylon and then Haran in modern Turkey near Syria, headed for his inheritance from God in the Promised Land of Canaan. In v. 8, what phrases highlight Abraham's confident faith in God?

c) Abraham believed God's covenant promise of land even though he never owned any of the Promised Land except his wife Sarah's burial plot. In v. 9, what phrase confirms that the patriarchs remained nomads and never permanently settled in Canaan?

d) The physical land of Canaan was a symbol of something even better. In v. 10 and 13-16, where was Abraham's ultimate destination, his true inheritance? How does it comfort you to realize that all believers are ultimately headed like Abraham for a better, permanent, heavenly homeland?

4. Abraham and His Descendants

In v. 11, scholars debate whether the author meant to say it was Sarah or Abraham who had faith in God's covenant promise of descendants. The original Greek says "Sarah." However, the power to conceive (literally "power for the laying down of seed") referred to a man's role, not a woman's role. In addition, Scripture records Sarah's doubt, not faith. Since Abraham could be the implied subject of this verse, a few translators give Abraham credit for faith instead of Sarah.

In any event, the point is that Sarah and Abraham persevered in faith even though they did not live to see fulfillment of the promise of numerous descendants. It was enough for them that God miraculously enabled their old bodies to produce Isaac, the son of the covenant.

a) In v. 13, how many patriarchs saw God's covenant promises fulfilled in their lifetime?

b) Read Romans 4:18-25. Like the author of Hebrews, Paul indicates that Abraham's body was as good as dead before conceiving Isaac. Abraham had faith that God would bring life to his body. How does Paul relate this to our faith in Jesus' resurrection?

Read Hebrews 11:17-22

5. Abraham's Greatest Test

Abraham's faith was severely tested when God told him to sacrifice Isaac, the only son of the promise. Jews today read the account of the binding of Isaac during the synagogue celebration of Rosh Hashanah, the Jewish new year. Jewish rabbinic tradition says Isaac was thirty-seven years old at the time of testing.

a) In v. 17, how did Abraham respond to God's command to sacrifice Isaac?

b) In v. 18, why would the sacrifice of Isaac have been such a momentous test of Abraham's faith in God's covenant promise of descendants?

c) In v. 19, what did Abraham believe about God?

d) Read Matthew 22:31-32. When Jesus said that the God of Abraham, Isaac, and Jacob is the God of the living, not the dead, what was He implying about the patriarchs?

e) As an adult in the prime of life, Isaac would have been strong enough to resist being sacrificed by Abraham who was a hundred years older than Isaac. Instead, Isaac knowingly consented to be sacrificed in obedience to God's will. Why is Isaac appropriately called a type or forerunner of Jesus Christ?

6. Other Patriarchs' Confident Faith

a) God renewed the Abrahamic covenant promises with Isaac. In v. 20, how did Isaac demonstrate confidence that God would care for his sons Jacob and Esau? Although both sons did prosper, the covenant promises were continued through Jacob.

b) God renewed the Abrahamic covenant promises with Isaac's son Jacob, also called Israel. In v. 21, how did Jacob demonstrate confidence that God would care for his son Joseph's sons, Manasseh and Ephraim?

c) In v. 22, how did Joseph show confident faith that God would fulfill His covenant promise of land? Four hundred years later, who made sure that Joseph's bones were carried to the Promised Land of Canaan during the Exodus out of Egypt (see Exodus 13:17-19)?

d) What do you find inspiring about the faith of the patriarchs?

Part III: Personal Application and Growth

Today's lesson points to several important truths that apply to our personal lives. Allow these truths to penetrate your mind, soften your heart, deepen your faith and affect your behavior to help you continually grow in Christ.

1. Faith is the assurance of things hoped for, the conviction of things not seen.

We can be inspired by the confident example of modern believers such as a woman named Jenny. Jenny says she spent a lot of time in her younger years asking God why He made her with Down Syndrome, but as her faith in Christ matured she came to see her life differently. She now recognizes that God has a special plan for her life that can only be carried out the way He made her.

Jenny says if she spends her time wishing she were different, she will not have time to do what God wants her to do. Besides being involved with work, church, and volunteering at a local hospital, she has encouraged thousands of people by sharing her faith testimony on television and other media. She delights in showing the love of Jesus and expressing her hope and joy in Him.[74]

How will *your* testimony reflect your joy, assurance, and hope in Christ?

2. We should imitate the confident faith of past believers.

Choose one or two heroes of the faith named in this lesson and become more familiar with their stories by reading the Scripture where they are recorded. What aspect of their confident faith will you imitate, starting right away?

3. The patriarchs believed God without seeing fulfillment in their lifetimes.

Jesus Christ is the fulfillment of God's promise to make Abraham's offspring a blessing to the world. Jesus continues to bless the world through the earthly ministry of His body, the true descendants of Abraham, the church. How will you personally take part in your church's efforts to bless the world?

Part IV: Closing Devotion
by Charles Spurgeon

Believer, behold the epitaph of all those blessed saints who fell asleep before the coming of our Lord! *"These all died in faith"* (Hebrews 11:13). It matters nothing how else they died, whether of old age or by violent means; this one point is the most worthy of record.

In faith they lived—it was their comfort, their guide, their motive and their support; and in the same spiritual grace they died, ending their life-song in the sweet strain in which they had so long continued. They held to the way of faith to the end.

Dying in faith has reference to the *past.* They believed the promises which had gone before, and were assured that their sins were blotted out through the mercy of God. Dying in faith has to do with the *present.* These saints were confident of their acceptance with God; they enjoyed the beams of His love and rested in His faithfulness. Dying in faith looks to the *future.* They fell asleep affirming that the Messiah would surely come.

Take courage, my soul, as you read this epitaph. Your course, through grace, is one of faith; this has also been the pathway of the brightest and the best. Thank Jesus for giving you the same precious faith with souls now in glory.[75]

∾ Lesson 20 ∽

Courageous Faith

Hebrews 11:23-40

Part I: Setting the Stage

Purpose

This lesson continues to look at the heroes of the faith in Hebrews 11, concentrating on the courageous faith of Moses, the judges, kings and prophets. It is important for us to imitate the faith of Old Testament believers who displayed courage in the face of danger or difficulty. Like them we are called to live bravely for God in a hostile world, knowing that in the end He will bring us to glory because of the saving work of Jesus Christ.

Look for the following application points in this lesson:

1. We should imitate the courageous faith of past believers.
2. Jesus Christ is the fulfillment of God's saving promises.
3. Old and New Testament believers together form one people of God.

The Second Major Group: Courageous Heroes

This lesson will look at the second major group of Old Testament heroes from the time of Moses to the prophets. See the Endnotes for specific Scripture references pertaining to the heroes of the faith in this lesson.[76]

The Bible is nearly silent about the centuries when the Hebrews were in bondage in Egypt. We do know that during that time the Hebrew people multiplied. Sometime after 1500 B.C. God called Moses to courageously continue what the patriarch Abraham had begun. Moses was to shape God's chosen people into a great nation set apart for God.

Moses led the Hebrews out of Egypt, delivered the Law, and brought God's people through the wilderness to the Promised Land of Canaan. His successor Joshua began the task of conquering and settling Canaan. During the next several centuries, the Israelites were governed by military judges such as Gideon, Barak, Samson and Jephthah. After that, Israel was ruled by kings until the Exile. God also sent prophets to advise the kings and people.

Why These and Not Those?
One question commonly asked about the second half of Hebrews 11 is why certain heroes are mentioned while others are left out. For instance, the prostitute Rahab of Jericho is depicted as a hero, but the godly leader Joshua who led the battle of Jericho is omitted. The scoundrel judges Samson and Jephthah are named as heroes, while the model judges Othniel and Ehud are excluded. Why these and not those?

Based on the author's purposeful arguments in the rest of Hebrews, there is no doubt that the named heroes in Hebrews 11 were carefully chosen. Perhaps the author wanted to highlight a variety of people and situations. He talks about righteous heroes who maintained confident faith in the unseen things of God. He presents flawed heroes who displayed courageous faith in spite of their own weakness or dangerous circumstances.

In Hebrews we see that God can use all kinds of people to accomplish His saving purposes. Fortunately, we do not have to be perfect to serve God.

One Household of God
The Old Testament heroes remind us there is only one household of God consisting of all of God's people from every age in history (Hebrews 3). God's house has been constructed during two building periods, the Old and New Testament eras. There is unity in God's household, for the promises given to believing national Israel under the old covenant were inherited by the true Israel, the church, in the new covenant.

As Hebrews 11 draws to a close the author makes it clear that Old and New Testament believers need each other in order for the church, the body of Christ, to be complete:

> "And all these [Old Testament heroes], though commended through their faith, did not receive what was promised, since God had provided something better for us, that apart from us they should not be made perfect." (Hebrews 11:39-40)

Old Testament believers received God's *promises* of salvation, and New Testament believers, including us, have seen the *fulfillment* of those promises. Together we are made complete in Christ and together we await the ultimate perfection that will accompany Christ's second coming. It is encouraging to know that God's plan for building His universal church will one day be brought to completion.

Part II: Studying Scripture

Read Hebrews 11:23-29

Moses is a giant among Old Testament heroes. Moses' life can be divided into three periods of forty years each: a prince of Egypt, a shepherd in Midian, and the lawgiver of Israel.

1. Moses in Egypt

a) In v. 23, how did Moses' parents show faith in God's protection?

b) In v. 24-25, at age forty Moses gave up the privilege of being a prince of Egypt, and chose instead to identify with the mistreatment of his fellow Hebrews. How would Moses' willingness to give up wealth encourage the persecuted readers of the book of Hebrews?

c) What choices have you had to make between the riches of the world and Christ? In what ways have those decisions strengthened your faith?

d) Moses had to decide which inheritance he treasured most: being a son of Pharaoh's daughter or a son of God's covenant. It was more than a matter of wealth and position; it was a spiritual crisis. Identifying with the Hebrew people meant identifying with their Messiah (Christ) and His disgrace. What reproach or disgrace did Christ endure? How do we share His disgrace today?

2. Moses and the Exodus

a) In v. 27, the reference to leaving Egypt by faith probably means the Exodus, not an earlier episode when Moses fearfully fled after killing an Egyptian. Why did Moses have courage to leave Egypt in the Exodus, unafraid of Pharaoh?

b) In v. 28, while preparing for the Exodus, how did Moses show faith in God's promise to pass over the houses of the Hebrews during the plague of death to the firstborn in Egypt?

c) In v. 29, how did the Israelites show courageous faith when they crossed the Red Sea after the Exodus out of Egypt?

d) The Exodus was God's main saving act of the Old Testament. It prepared God's people for His greatest saving act of all time in Christ. Why do you think God gave His people a foreshadowing of what He was going to do in Christ?

e)   People do not need to study the Old Testament before coming to Christ. However, after conversion a better knowledge of the Old Testament increases our understanding of what Jesus Christ has done for us. How do you plan to keep growing in your knowledge of the Old Testament?

Read Hebrews 11:30-31

3.   Entering Canaan

a)   At the beginning of the conquest of Canaan, the Israelites believed God's promise of victory at Jericho and were obedient to His commands. In v. 30, what was the result of the Israelites' faith?

b)   The Canaanite prostitute Rahab believed God and proved her allegiance by hiding the Israelite spies in Jericho. In v. 31, what was the result of Rahab's bold faith?

c)   Think of a time when you exhibited faith in the face of danger. What was the result?

Read Hebrews 11:32-40

4.   Living in Canaan

The next six characters illustrate victorious faith in spite of obstacles. Each pair of characters shares a similar type of faith. Within each pair the author reverses the order of their appearance in the Old Testament, perhaps to draw our attention to them as a pair.

a) Gideon and Barak: Hesitant Faith

When God called Gideon to be a judge, Gideon hesitated to lead an army without God's repeated assurances of success. Gideon finally responded in faith and God gave him victory.

The judge Barak needed reassurance about God's word through the judge Deborah. Barak proved to be faithful and God gave him and Deborah victory together.

How can you learn to believe God's word with more confidence, without testing Him or requiring further assurances?

b) Samson and Jephthah: Reckless Faith

The judge Samson was impulsive, violent, and had a reputation for being a self-centered womanizer. In the end, though, he allowed God to use him to defeat the Philistines at Gaza by himself, knowing he would die in the effort.

The judge Jephthah was a rash, self-interested outcast who is probably best remembered for making a foolish and fatal vow, but he allowed God to use him to defeat the Ammonites to save Israel.

Knowing that God can use less than perfect people like these to accomplish His saving purposes, how does it give you encouragement that God can use you, too? How have you made yourself available for God to use? What changes will you make in order to be more available to Him?

c) David and Samuel: Devoted Faith

David was the greatest king of Israel. Although his sinful deeds are well documented in Scripture, so is his heartfelt repentance to God. David sought to keep Israel faithful to God.

Samuel was the last judge of Israel, a great man chosen by God to anoint Saul and David, the first two kings of Israel. Samuel encouraged Israel to remain true to God.

From your own observation of honorable people who take their faith seriously, what positive things will you imitate about the way they respond to sin and other challenges in their lives?

5. Victories and Sufferings

a) From the list in v. 33-35, what were some of the ways Israel's faithful judges, kings and prophets enjoyed victories in the following categories:[77]

Dominion: _____

Safety: _____

Strength: _____

Resurrection: _____

b) Confident and courageous faith will not always lead to victories. We must be prepared to suffer for our faith. From the list in v. 35-38, what were some of the hardships endured by Israel's godly leaders in the following categories:[78]

Suffering: _____

Murder: _____

Poverty: _____

c) In modern times, Pastor Richard Wurmbrand, founder of The Voice of the Martyrs, suffered for his faith as a pastor in Communist Romania. He was imprisoned and tortured for fourteen years before being ransomed:

> "I tremble because of the sufferings of those persecuted in different lands. I tremble thinking about the eternal destiny of their torturers. I tremble for Western Christians who don't help their persecuted brethren. In the depth of my heart, I would like to keep the beauty of my own vineyard and not be involved in such a huge fight. I would like so much to be somewhere in quietness and rest. But it is not possible... The quietness and rest for which I long would be an escape from reality and dangerous for my soul... The West sleeps and must be awakened to see the plight of the captive nations."[79]

What steps will you take to become more aware of and involved in caring for persecuted brothers and sisters in Christ?

6. Made Perfect Together With Us

a) In v. 39, faithful Old Testament believers had God's promises, but what was missing?

b) In v. 40, what do you think is the "better" thing God provided for New Testament believers, so that Old and New Testament believers together are made perfect, meaning complete?

c) Believers from the Old Testament era had the promise of salvation, and believers from the New Testament era have fulfillment of that promise in Christ. Promise and fulfillment go together. How would you explain to a new Christian that Old and New Testament believers need each other and are incomplete without sharing in what the other has?

Part III: Personal Application and Growth

Today's lesson points to several important truths that apply to our personal lives. Allow these truths to penetrate your mind, soften your heart, deepen your faith and affect your behavior to help you continually grow in Christ.

1. We should imitate the courageous faith of past believers.

Choose one or two heroes of the faith named in this lesson and become more familiar with their stories by reading the Scripture where they are recorded. What aspect of their courageous faith will you emulate, starting right away?

2. Jesus Christ is the fulfillment of God's saving promises.

How will you demonstrate to people around you what it looks like to live every day in the joy of the age of fulfillment?

3. Old and New Testament believers together form one people of God.

In what ways will the hope of living forever with believers from throughout history give you energy and purpose this week?

Part IV: Closing Devotion
by Charles Spurgeon

Believer, it is a delightful and profitable occupation to notice the hand of God in the lives of ancient saints, and to observe His goodness in delivering them, His mercy in pardoning them, and His faithfulness in keeping His covenant with them.

But would it not be even more interesting and profitable for us to notice the hand of God in our own lives? Ought we not to look upon our own history as being at least as full of God, as full of His goodness and of His truth, as much a proof of His faithfulness, as the lives of any of the saints who have gone before?

Let us review our lives. Surely we may discover some happy incidents refreshing to ourselves and glorifying to God. Have you had deliverance? Special favors? Green pastures and still waters? Surely the goodness of God has been the same to us as to the saints of old.

Let us take the pure gold of thankfulness and the jewels of praise and make them into another crown for the head of Jesus. Let our souls give forth music as sweet and exhilarating as came from David's harp, while we praise the Lord whose mercy endures forever.[80]

ॐ Lesson 21 ॐ

Enduring Hope

Hebrews 12:1-17

Part I: Setting the Stage

Purpose

This lesson compares living the Christian life to running a long-distance race. As we run we are to maintain enduring hope in Christ without growing weary, and we are to allow God's discipline to make us stronger so we finish the race well. It is important for us to look to Jesus, the one who has run the race perfectly and makes it possible for us to follow Him into heaven.

Look for the following application points in this lesson:

1. We are to put our hope in Jesus Christ.
2. Suffering can be a means of discipline to help us grow toward spiritual maturity.
3. Christians are meant to finish the race of life well, persevering in faith to the end.

Perseverance of the Saints

One of the central doctrines of our faith is called the perseverance of the saints. This doctrine teaches that true believers (saints) will never lose their salvation, because God will see to it that they persevere in faith to the end of life. Sometimes this doctrine is called the preservation of the saints because God preserves true believers to the end.

This is not the counterfeit doctrine of eternal security that says once saved, always saved, meaning that a person can confess Christ but then live in deliberate, defiant sin and reject God permanently without losing salvation. That false doctrine goes against Scripture.

Rather, saving faith is evidenced by good works and a desire for holy living. The *Westminster Confession of Faith* affirms the doctrine of the perseverance of the saints:

> "They, whom God hath accepted in His Beloved, effectually called, and sanctified by His Spirit, can neither totally nor finally fall away from the state of grace, but shall certainly persevere therein to the end, and be eternally saved."[81]

Training for the Race

One of the ways we are enabled to persevere in faith is by rigorous training that strengthens us. God's training program is not for the faint of heart. He disciplines those He loves for the purpose of building their endurance and strength, and His discipline can seem harsh. The author of Hebrews encourages us to remember that when we face suffering we should see it as discipline and training to build endurance for the race.

The author's argument is that a good father disciplines his children. We can be grateful that God considers us to be heirs worthy of His proper discipline and training. Whether or not we understand His methods, we are to allow the pain and suffering of persecution to produce holiness and righteousness in our lives. Our suffering is made more bearable when we remember what Jesus suffered for us. Focusing on Jesus will help us endure to the end.

Keeping Our Eyes on the Prize

An example of the importance of an athlete staying focused on the end goal comes from the experience of renowned swimmer Florence May Chadwick. In 1952 Chadwick made an attempt to swim from Catalina Island to the California coastline, a distance of twenty-six miles. She set out accompanied by small boats that kept a watch out for sharks and were prepared to give her assistance if she got hurt or grew tired.

After about fifteen hours a thick fog set in and Chadwick began to doubt whether she could finish. She swam for another hour but could not see the coastline in the fog and finally asked to be pulled into one of the boats. As she sat there she realized she had given up less than a mile from her destination. Fortunately, the story does not end there:

> "Two months later, Chadwick tried again. This time was different. The same thick fog set in, but she made it because she said that she kept a mental image of the shoreline in her mind while she swam."[82]

Let us keep the true reality of Jesus Christ and our heavenly destination in our mind while we run the good race.

Part II: Studying Scripture

Read Hebrews 12:1-2

Old Testament heroes of the faith had God's saving promises but died without receiving fulfillment. Those of us in the New Testament era have the fulfillment of God's promises in Jesus Christ. Believers from all periods of time are bound together forever by God's saving promises and fulfillment.

The author uses athletic language to express this bond, picturing the Christian life as a long-distance race. The Greek word for race (*agon*) implies endurance, agony, struggle, and conflict. It takes constant effort and forward motion. We are to imagine ourselves in an athletic stadium filled with witnesses (*martys*, from which we get the word "martyrs") who want us to finish well for our sake and theirs. They are made complete only together with all the believers.

1. Follow the Course

a) In v. 1, what do you think it means that our race is "set before us" or marked out for us? Who marks the course for us?

b) Jesus also ran the race that was "set before Him." God set the course for Jesus just as He does for us. In v. 2, what course did God choose for Jesus?

c) The author rarely speaks of the specifics of Jesus' life on earth and here he mentions the cross for the first and only time. In v. 2, what was Jesus' reward for enduring the cross?

2. Run With Endurance

Give specific examples of the following ways to keep the faith as we run:

Lay aside every weight or hindrance: _____

_____

Lay aside every sin that clings or entangles: _____

_____

Run with endurance and perseverance: _____

_____

Look to Jesus and fix our eyes on Him: _____

_____

3. Focus on the End Goal

a) Because Jesus finished His earthly race well He makes it possible for us to finish well. In v. 2, what do you think it means that Jesus is the founder or author of our faith?

b) Why is it essential that Jesus is the perfecter or finisher of our faith as well?

c)   We are to focus our attention not on ourselves or the witnesses, but on Jesus. Although we can never live perfectly as Jesus did, what are some of the things we should imitate about the way Jesus ran His race?

d)   We should keep our eyes fixed on where we want to go. What happens when an athlete loses focus of the end goal during a race?

e)   As we run our race, how can we keep our eyes on Jesus even though He is hidden from our view in heaven?

Read Hebrews 12:3-11

4.   Accept God's Discipline

a)   The readers have been persecuted, but not yet to the point of bloodshed. It is possible, though, that if they are in Rome they will face martyrdom under Emperor Nero starting in A.D. 64. In v. 3-4, whatever their level of persecution, how will it strengthen their faith to consider the hostility Jesus endured? How does it strengthen your faith to consider His endurance?

b)   In v. 5, what two extreme reactions to discipline should we avoid? Why would these reactions prevent us from receiving the benefits of God's discipline?

c) The author quotes a well-known proverb about divine discipline (Proverbs 3:11-12, Septuagint version). In v. 6b, the word for "chastise" or punish means scourging, being beaten with a multistranded spiked whip. The image is harsh and we must consider it in context. According to v. 6, why does God discipline us? How does this ensure that His chastisement is restrained and designed for our ultimate good?

d) In v. 7-8, a Roman nobleman would raise his legal heir at home with discipline, but an illegitimate son would live elsewhere without his father's guidance. When we refuse God's discipline, in effect which son's status are we identifying with? Why does this insult God?

e) Jesus, the Son of God, received His inheritance through suffering. How do v. 7-8 prepare us to expect the same thing?

5. Be Trained By Discipline

a) In v. 9-10, the author argues from the lesser to the greater. Since we generally respect an earthly father's discipline as a means of learning how to live right, we should respect our perfect heavenly Father's discipline even more. In v. 10, what are some ways earthly fathers are limited and fallible? Why is God's discipline superior?

b) Unfortunately, not all believers can say they respect their earthly fathers with regard to discipline. If your childhood discipline was too harsh or too lax, let Jesus redeem it by bringing something positive from it. What helpful things have you learned as a result of the way you were raised? How will you allow your experience to make you compassionate and reasonable with the children in your life?

c) The purpose of athletic discipline is to build endurance and train the body and mind in order to achieve results. The author mixes athletic and agricultural metaphors to make his point. We are trained (*gymnazo*), like gymnasts, in order to produce a harvest of fruit. The metaphors are not as odd a mix as it might seem. Sometimes an unproductive fruit tree needs its branches pruned or needs blunt force to the trunk to stimulate the production of fruit.

In v. 11, what should be the result of our being trained by God's discipline or chastening?

d) What do you find comforting about the idea that God's painful discipline can produce peaceful righteousness if we let it? How will this idea help you face adversity?

Read Hebrews 12:12-17

6. Strive for Peace and Holiness

a) In v. 12, the author offers a proof text from the prophet Isaiah who proclaimed that God's oppressed people should not fear, for God would save them (Isaiah 35:3). When we react to persecution and other forms of God's discipline with fear, what should we do according to this verse? How does the peaceful righteousness of v. 11 help us shake off the fear and renew our strength?

b) We should also avoid future spiritual injury. In v. 13, the author's proof text is from a collection of fatherly instructions (Proverbs 4:26). Being lame is a metaphor for being weak in faith. Why should we make our paths morally straight and in line with God's righteousness, especially when our faith is weak?

c) In v. 14-15a, the author explains his metaphor more plainly. What should we strive for? Why would it require special effort for persecuted readers to live in peace with everyone?

d) In v. 15b-16, what are some major obstacles to peace within the body of Christ? The people being described here may be attending church but do not show evidence of God's saving grace.

e) Why is it the church's business if a member is involved in sexual immorality? In other words, how do allegedly private sins like adultery, fornication (sex outside of traditional marriage between one man and one woman), and pornography negatively impact and dishonor the purity of the church, Christ's body?

f) In v. 16-17, Esau showed he was unholy by despising his birthright and rejecting the faith of his father Isaac and grandfather Abraham. Later Esau sought his father's blessing with weeping, but Esau was hardened and for him true repentance was impossible. How can we minister to unholy people in our midst without being negatively influenced by their unholy attitude?

Part III: Personal Application and Growth

Today's lesson points to several important truths that apply to our personal lives. Allow these truths to penetrate your mind, soften your heart, deepen your faith and affect your behavior to help you continually grow in Christ.

1.   We are to put our hope in Jesus Christ.

What practical things will you do this week to look to Jesus and His saving work when disappointments, problems, distractions, and even successes take your focus off Him?

2.   Suffering can be a means of discipline to help us grow toward spiritual maturity.

We do not always know why God allows particular hardships in our lives. Sometimes He initiates a training program of discipline we did not ask for. Consider the difficulties that are currently causing you pain or suffering. How will you bring your attitude in line with God's so that you allow suffering to strengthen the muscles of your faith?

3.   Christians are meant to finish the race of life well, persevering in faith to the end.

Think of someone currently in your life who has kept the faith into old age. This week arrange to visit and listen to the story of his or her faith journey. What questions will you ask? How do you think such a visit will be a blessing to both of you?

Part IV: Closing Devotion
by Charles Spurgeon

Believer, it is ever the Holy Spirit's work to turn our eyes away from self to Jesus; but Satan's work is just the opposite of this, for he is constantly trying to make us regard ourselves instead of Christ. He insinuates, "Your sins are too great for pardon; you have no faith; you do not repent enough; you will never be able to continue to the end; you have not the joy of His children." All these are thoughts about self, and we shall never find comfort or assurance by looking within.

But the Holy Spirit turns our eyes entirely away from self: He tells us that Christ is all in all. Therefore, look not to your hope, but to Jesus, the source of your hope; look not to your faith, but to Jesus, the author and finisher of your faith. We shall never find happiness by looking at our prayers, our doings, or our feelings; it is what *Jesus* is, not what we are, that gives rest to the soul.

Keep your eye simply on Him; let His death, His sufferings, His merits, His glories, His intercession, be fresh upon your mind; when you wake in the morning look to Him; when you lie down at night look to Him. Oh! Let not your hopes or fears come between you and Jesus; follow close after Him and He will never fail you.[83]

❧ Lesson 22 ❦

Unshakable Hope

Hebrews 12:18-29

Part I: Setting the Stage

Purpose

This lesson urges us to maintain unshakable hope in Jesus Christ as we run the race of life toward heaven, our finish line. Heaven is the invisible but true reality where Christ lives and mediates the new covenant. It is important for us to know that our hope of salvation is unshakable because Christ, the object of our hope, is unshakable. The kingdom of God the Father, Son, and Holy Spirit is unshakable and will endure forever.

Look for the following application points in this lesson:

1. The old covenant of law pointed to death; the new covenant of grace points to life.
2. Our hope of salvation is unshakable because Christ's kingdom is unshakable.
3. We should respond to God with reverent worship.

Heaven Now

Since the destination of the Christian life is heaven, it is worth our time to explore the concept of heaven a bit more. One question people frequently ask is whether heaven is an actual place.

Scripture indicates that heaven is a place with some sort of spatial quality. Perhaps it exists in a dimension not yet known to us. It is referred to as being up or away from the earth, beyond the stars and cosmos. Jesus lives in heaven right now in His resurrection body, a mysterious version of His earthly body. The souls or spirits of all dead believers (saints) are also in heaven, waiting for the day they will be reunited with their resurrected earthly bodies.

The Bible gives us glimpses of the present state of heaven, but there is a great deal we will never know during this lifetime. Biblical characters who experienced visions of heaven or first-hand visitation such as Isaiah, Paul, John, and others found themselves unable to fully describe their experience by means of limited human language.

Heaven Later
When Jesus returns at the end times, He will complete the renewal of Creation which began at His first coming.[84] The final upheaval will involve war, fiery destruction of the world, renewal of the whole universe, change, replacement, and judgment. The physical bodies of all dead people will be resurrected to join their souls for eternity either in heaven or hell.

Heaven, the New Jerusalem, will descend to earth at the end times and God will dwell among humanity forever (Revelation 21:2-3). It will truly be heaven on earth. We can think of it as both a restoration of the original situation in the Garden of Eden and also something greater and completely new.

Christianity does not share the popular belief that matter is inherently bad and that the ideal existence is only spiritual. The Christian view is that the ideal existence entails God's transformation and perfection of our physical bodies and world, not escape from them. We look forward to the immortality of the whole person, both body and spirit together.

The Kingdom of Heaven
We should note that there are different uses of the word heaven. As we have seen, heaven normally refers to the unseen place where Jesus now bodily lives. The plural word heavens usually means the cosmos or outer space, although there are exceptions.

On the other hand, the kingdom of heaven, also called the kingdom of God or kingdom of Christ, is the reign of God. It is not a place limited by space or time. At Jesus' first coming the kingdom of heaven broke into the world, and the kingdom will be consummated at Jesus' second coming. Thus Jesus spoke in terms of the kingdom having arrived and not yet having arrived (Luke 4:17-21; Matthew 12:28-29; Matthew 6:10).

The time between Christ's two comings has lasted over two thousand years and is often referred to as "the already and the not yet," or in more technical terms, "realized and unrealized eschatology." During this time we can be encouraged that although things are not as good as they will be some day, they are not as bad as they could be. Christ has bound the strong man Satan and limited his activity until Christ's final return and victory. God reigns and His kingdom is eternal and unshakable.

Part II: Studying Scripture

Read Exodus 19:9-13, 16-19

1.   Mediating the Old Covenant of Law

When the Israelites left Egypt in the Exodus, Moses did not take them directly to Canaan. Instead he led them south to Mount Sinai to receive God's law and establish Israel's national identity. The proof text from Exodus 19 is a reminder that the old covenant of law was mediated in an atmosphere of gloom at Mount Sinai.

a)   In v. 9, what did God tell Moses to expect with regard to His visible appearance on Mount Sinai? What was the purpose of God's manifestation?

b)   In v. 10-13, what did the rituals of purity and the limited access to the mountain teach people about God's holiness?

c) God led the Israelites in the Exodus by His presence in the pillars of cloud and fire. The episode at Mount Sinai was a similar theophany, a visible manifestation of God. Commentators observe that the details cannot be completely explained by natural phenomena such as volcanic activity or an earthquake. List several elements described in v. 16-19. What effect do you think God's manifestation had on the Israelites?

Read Hebrews 12:18-21

2. Earthly Mount Sinai

"For you have not come to what may be touched..." The original Greek does not use the word mountain, but the readers would have immediately recognized the author's reference to Mount Sinai where Moses mediated the old covenant of Law.

a) The old covenant was mediated by Moses under terrifying conditions. If you had been at Mount Sinai then, which condition would have been most fearful to you?

b) If you were to sum up the mood at Mount Sinai, what three words would you use?

c) Moses had fearlessly spoken with God many times before Mount Sinai. Why do you think God manifested Himself now in such a terrifying way that even Moses was afraid?

Read Hebrews 12:22-24

3.   Heavenly Mount Zion

"But you have come to..." Using symbolic language, the author refers to the sanctuary in heaven as the heavenly Mount Zion and heavenly city Jerusalem. These fitting metaphors evoke the earthly Temple located on Mount Zion, the highest elevation in Jerusalem. During our lifetime we arrive at the heavenly Mount Zion spiritually, not bodily.

a)   Mediation of the new covenant is described in contrast to the old covenant. Based on v. 22-24, describe the atmosphere of heaven in your own words.

b)   The author earlier said Abel's faithful worship still speaks to us (Hebrews 11:4). Now we read that Abel's shed blood also speaks, calling for God's vengeance under the old covenant (Genesis 4:9-10). The original Greek in our passage does not say "the blood of" Abel, but it is implied. In contrast, what does Jesus' shed blood of the new covenant call for (Hebrews 9:12-15)?

c)   The chart below summarizes the mediation of the old covenant by Moses and the new covenant by Jesus. Which contrast stands out most to you?

Mediating the Covenants

	Old Covenant (v. 18-21)	New Covenant (v. 22-24)
Location	Visible, earthly Mt. Sinai	Invisible, heavenly Mt. Zion
Atmosphere	Dark, gloom, fire, storm	Joy, angels, saints, Jesus
Provisions	Law, judgment, death	Salvation, mercy, life
Result	Distance from God, fear	Nearness to God, confidence

---

d) Under the old covenant, firstborn males were consecrated to serve God but the Levites redeemed them and served in their place. In the new covenant, all true believers have firstborn status and are enrolled in heaven as those consecrated to serve God.

In v. 23, the "assembly of the firstborn" could mean all believers, but it probably refers to believers living on earth. "Spirits of the righteous" probably refers to dead believers whose souls are in heaven. In what practical ways will you show respect for the firstborn status of Christians in denominations besides your own?

Read Hebrews 12:25-29

4. A Shakable World

The argument moves from the lesser to the greater. If escape from punishment was impossible for those who disobeyed the old covenant revealed by God at Mount Sinai, then escape is certainly impossible for those who disobey His new covenant revealed from heaven.

a) In v. 26, the author quotes a messianic proof text from the prophet Haggai who predicted that God would someday again shake the earth and the heavens (Haggai 2:6). How was the prophecy partially fulfilled at the inauguration of the new covenant when Jesus died? (See Matthew 27:51 and 28:2)

b) Long-term messianic fulfillment of Haggai's prophecy will occur at the end times when Jesus Christ returns in final consummation of the new covenant. What will be the glorious result of God's shaking the earth and heavens then? (See Romans 8:18-21; Revelation 21:1)

c) Why do you think God long ago foretold the radical changes He would make? How does it strengthen your faith to know these predictions will surely be fulfilled?

5. An Unshakable Kingdom

a) In v. 27, what will happen to things that have been shaken? What about things that cannot be shaken?

b) In v. 28, what will remain? How should we respond?

c) Read Hebrews 1:10-12. What image or simile does the author employ to describe shakable things that will perish and be changed?

d) The kingdom of heaven, also called the kingdom of God, has already broken into the world upon Jesus' first coming. Looking around, what evidence do you see that God's kingdom has arrived, at least in part?

6. Offering Acceptable Worship

a) In v. 28, why do you suppose reverence as well as awe or godly fear are essential attitudes in worship? In your experience, what happens to worship when we downplay these attitudes too much?

b) In v. 29, the author quotes a proof text to remind us that God will not tolerate idolatry (Deuteronomy 4:23-24). What do you think it means that God is a consuming fire? Whom does God consume? (See Deuteronomy 8:19-20; 9:3-4; Matthew 25:41-46)

c) Why would our divided loyalty offend God so much? Where do you see divided loyalty to God in your own worship? What will you do to change that?

d) Read Galatians 6:7-8. Unbelievers should not think they will escape God's eternal judgment. Why do you think so many people mock God or treat Him carelessly?

e) Scientist Francis Collins, Director of the National Institutes of Health (NIH), admits he was a rather outspoken atheist before his conversion to Christianity at age twenty-seven. He considered religion to be a superstitious carryover from a pre-scientific age rendered irrelevant by the scientific age of reason. His mission was to convince others that nothing existed except what could be measured.[85]

As a medical resident Collins witnessed the power of faith in certain patients and decided to learn more about what he was rejecting. He discovered C. S. Lewis' writings and found himself won over by Lewis' argument for the existence of the moral law. The moral law in our hearts tells us there is a God who is good, holy, and perfect. When we realize our own imperfection, the Holy Spirit helps us see that we need Jesus Christ to bring God and us together.

Why is it important to have ongoing conversations about God with our atheist friends? What can we do to demonstrate our respect and awe for God in such a way that they become curious to know more about Him?

Part III: Personal Application and Growth

Today's lesson points to several important truths that apply to our personal lives. Allow these truths to penetrate your mind, soften your heart, deepen your faith and affect your behavior to help you continually grow in Christ.

1. The old covenant of law pointed to death; the new covenant of grace points to life.

Starting today, what changes will you make in your television and online viewing habits to foster positive, life-affirming attitudes with an eternal perspective? How do you think this might improve your relationships?

2. Our hope of salvation is unshakable because Christ's kingdom is unshakable.

Ask a few non-Christians this week what they think will last forever. Be ready to explain the Christian view that God's kingdom is the only thing that will last, including its spiritual and physical elements. If they do not believe in God, ask if they will be open-minded about the possibility that He exists and wants us to have life with Him after death. Invite them to your church to hear more if they are willing.

3. We should respond to God with reverent worship.

Starting today, how will your prayers and worship express increased reverence for God? What adjustments will you make in your everyday language to honor God more?

Part IV: Closing Devotion
by Charles Spurgeon

Believer, we have many things in our possession at the present moment which can be shaken. Yet, we have certain things which cannot be shaken, and I invite you to think of them, so that if the things which can be shaken should all be taken away, you may derive real comfort from the things that cannot be shaken, which will remain.

Whatever your losses may be, you enjoy *present salvation*. You are trusting in the merit of Jesus' precious blood only. No rise or fall of the markets can interfere with your salvation in Him; no breaking of banks, no failures and bankruptcies can touch that.

Then you are a child of God, *God is your Father*. No change of circumstances can ever rob you of that. Although losses may bring you to poverty, you can say, "He is my Father still. In my Father's house are many mansions; therefore I will not be troubled."

You have another permanent blessing, namely, the *love of Jesus Christ*. He who is God and Man loves you with all His affectionate nature – nothing can affect that. Whatever troubles come, our hope is above the sky. Rejoice in the God of our salvation![86]

❧ Lesson 23 ❦

Brotherly Love

Hebrews 13:1-19

Part I: Setting the Stage

Purpose

This lesson reminds us to show brotherly and sisterly love to believers in order to help each other persevere in faith and thereby strengthen the church, the body of Christ. Our fellow Christians need daily encouragement, just as we need encouragement. It is important for us to remember that a mark of discipleship is the love Jesus' disciples have for one another.

Look for the following application points in this lesson:

1. We should put love into action to encourage one another in faith.
2. Our personal behavior affects the entire body of Christ, the church.
3. We are to pray for and support our church leaders.

Keeping the Faith

The overall purpose of Hebrews is encouragement to keep the faith. The author has encouraged us by addressing our whole being: mind, heart, and behavior.

First, the author laid out foundational truths about Jesus Christ. He also gave inspirational examples of men and women who believed God's saving promises without seeing fulfillment. He exhorted us to prove our faith to ourselves by persevering in hope and now he urges us to show brotherly love to each other. These points are listed below.

Our Whole Being

		<u>Chapter</u>
Mind	Know who Jesus Christ is and what He has done.	1-10
Heart	Be inspired by the faith of others.	11
Behavior	Practice faith with enduring hope and brotherly love.	12-13

A Mark of Discipleship

Hebrews 12 dealt mainly with our personal hope in Christ. In Hebrews 13 the author speaks about our love for other believers in the church. This communal aspect of faith is essential. Jesus set the standard, "By this all people will know that you are my disciples, if you have love for one another" (John 13:35). Paul exhorted, "So then, as we have opportunity, let us do good to everyone, and especially to those who are of the household of faith" (Galatians 6:10).

The author of Hebrews has already commended his readers for showing one another unconditional love, *agape* (Hebrews 6:10). Now he asks them to build up one another's faith by showing brotherly love, *philadelphia*.

Our Communal Responsibility

Some commentators think the acts of love listed in Hebrews 13 are a random addition of disconnected thoughts. One critic says the author inserted the list because he changed his mind about the kind of letter he wanted to write.[87] Is the author really so haphazard? No, far from it! He continues the orderly approach he has shown throughout the letter. We see his purpose and direction in this last chapter as in the rest of Hebrews.

At any given time, the church is under attack by hostile forces from without and within. Believers have a duty to watch over each other and guard the purity of the church. The author exhorts his readers to offer hospitality, support those being persecuted, hold each other accountable for sexual behavior, avoid financial corruption, obey and encourage church leaders, maintain sound doctrine, be generous with resources, do good works, and pray for those in ministry.

These are not random, unrelated issues, but represent vulnerable areas in a church, especially a young church with spiritually immature believers. The author understood that his readers needed to be diligent in these areas. Issues involving corruption, false doctrine, discouragement, money, sex, and power have been the downfall of countless ministries.

Some Christians would rather not get involved in a local church, but Scripture insists we have a responsibility to maintain fellowship and hold each other accountable for our behavior and beliefs. The author's exhortations and teachings are for the purpose of encouraging us to keep the faith and build up the body of Christ for the glory of God.

Part II: Studying Scripture

Read Hebrews 13:1-6

The author begins, "Let brotherly love (*philadelphia*) continue." Some see this as the first item in a list of behaviors Christians should exhibit toward all people. It seems more likely, though, to be a summary statement of the specifics that follow with regard to the way Christians should treat each other.

1. Mercy Ministry

a) The duty to show hospitality to strangers was a feature of the ancient near east at a time when inns were not always available, affordable, or safe. In v. 2, which Old Testament character was blessed because he entertained angels unawares? (See Genesis 18:1-11)

b) The readers are to entertain strangers, presumably including traveling missionaries and itinerant preachers. List several ways one can be hospitable in addition to opening up one's home. How have you been blessed by showing some form of hospitality to a missionary?

c) The Didache (DID-uh-kay) was a 1st century training manual for new Christians. It explained how to offer hospitality and yet recognize free-loaders:

> "Welcome every apostle on arriving, as if he were the Lord. But he must not stay beyond one day. In case of necessity, however, the next day, too. If he stays three days, he is a false prophet."[88]

Why was this a good test to discern a false prophet? What problems might arise when false prophets exploit a hospitable situation? How can such problems be avoided today?

d) Christians were to care for imprisoned and mistreated fellow believers. There are parts of the world today where prisoners still depend on relatives and friends to bring basic food, blankets and medicine for survival. In v. 3, why should we empathize with the physical needs of Christians persecuted by imprisonment and mistreatment? Note that the reference to the body probably means a physical body rather than the church, the body of Christ.

2. Sexual Purity

a) The author says marriage should be held in honor among all. Traditional marriage between one man and one woman is a Creation ordinance applicable to all people. What evidence do you see that traditional marriage is dishonored in our society today?

b) The author goes on to say that the marriage bed should be undefiled. This is a warning against sex outside traditional marriage. Other relationships of love or lust are not to be expressed sexually. In v. 4, what is the result of adultery and all kinds of sexual immorality?

c) Since the Bible holds traditional marriage to be the only acceptable venue for sex, most people are called to abstinence. Although this is an unpopular view today, sex is a marital privilege, not a human right. When a pastor publicly announces in a wedding ceremony that the groom may kiss the bride, it signifies the church's permission for the couple to be physically intimate now that they are married. How will you support your church's promotion of Biblical sexual standards?

d) Read Ephesians 5:31-32. What does the sacred union of traditional marriage ultimately represent? When people disregard, violate, or redefine marriage, why does it show disdain for Christ?

3. Financial Contentment

a) Financial advisor Howard Dayton urges us to be faithful stewards of God's property, get out of debt, give generously, budget, and work as unto the Lord. We are to handle our resources in light of eternity, the long tomorrow:

> "Our failure to view our present lives through the lens of eternity is one of the biggest hindrances to seeing our lives and our assets in their true light. Yet Scripture states that the reality of our eternal future should determine the character of our present lives and the use of our money and possessions."[89]

In v. 5, what attitudes toward money and material possessions should we have?

b) The context of the proof text in v. 5 is Joshua's preparation for the conquest of Canaan (Joshua 1:5). What is God's promise? How does His promise apply to you?

c) In v. 6, the proof text comes from David's confident declaration that God is in control and brings about the victory (Psalm 118:6-7). Note that the word "helper" (*ezer* in Hebrew) connotes a military ally. What confidence should we have?

d) Read I Timothy 6:10. Being greedy or discontent with what we have is a form of fear. We do not trust God to provide adequately; we are ungrateful for His provision; or we arrogantly judge Him to be unfair. When have you been fearful about God's provision? How do you plan to deal with your discontent?

Read Hebrews 13:7-16

4. Imitate Past Leaders

a) In v. 7, the first generation of leaders in the early church was passing away. What past ministry leader have you known and admired for persevering in faith until death? What aspect of his or her faith will you imitate?

b) Since even the best leaders eventually pass away, church leadership will change. In v. 8, who is the unchanging object of our faith? Why is it comforting that He is forever constant?

c) In v. 9, "diverse and strange teachings" might mean pagan worship, but more likely Levitical worship. Although Levitical teachings were not strange in the sense of being unfamiliar to the readers, such teachings were foreign to the new covenant. Instead of relying on old covenant Levitical sacrifices to obtain God's mercy, what do believers in the new covenant rely on?

d) In v. 10, commentators are divided as to whether our "altar" refers to the cross or Christ Himself. It is probably not a communion table, for that is not an altar. We figuratively eat from the altar by partaking in the blessings of complete forgiveness obtained in Christ. This contrasts sharply with Levitical priests. As long as they served under the old covenant, why did Levitical priests have no right to claim the blessings of Christ's death?

e) In v. 11, carcasses of sin sacrifices were removed from the people's presence because the bodies symbolically bore the people's sin and were therefore unclean. On the annual Day of Atonement, after the blood cleansed the holy places the animals' dead bodies were taken outside the camp. In v. 12, in a loose parallel with the Day of Atonement, Jesus bore the people's sin, His blood cleansed them, and His dead body was outside the camp or gates of Jerusalem.

Why would this parallel reassure readers they no longer needed Levitical sacrifices for atonement?

f) In v. 13, what should all believers expect when they put their faith in Jesus? What forms does this take? In v. 14, why won't we have to endure it forever?

g) There is no need for further blood sacrifices of atonement because Christ offered the final one. In v. 15-16, though, what sacrifices does God desire?

Read Hebrews 13:17-19

5. Obey Present Leaders

a) In v. 17, how should believers act toward their current church leaders? How should church leaders act toward their congregation?

b) Our attitudes and actions impact our church leaders more than we might think. We should not make their work a burden they bear with grief, literally "groaning." Look up the definition of the word "groan" in a dictionary and list the kinds of things that cause groaning.

c) How will you avoid doing things that cause groaning, and instead make it a joy for your pastor and church officers to serve? What is the advantage to you and the whole church when your leaders serve with joy?

d) The Reformer John Calvin says it is our duty to build up church leaders:

> "The author also bids us to be teachable and ready to obey, so that what pastors do in consequence of what their office demands, they may also willingly and *joyfully* do; for, if they have their minds restrained by grief or weariness, though they may be sincere and faithful, they will yet become disheartened and careless... Let us then remember that we are suffering the punishment of our own perverseness whenever the pastors grow cold in their duty or are less diligent than they ought to be."[90]

6. Pray for Absent Leaders

a) In v. 18, we do not know what kept the author apart from his readers. Perhaps the author was under threat of persecution by Jewish leaders opposed to his new covenant teaching. Although we do not know the exact problem the author faced, what defense does he offer?

b) How do you suppose the readers were to be specifically praying for their absent leaders? How can we support church leaders in other parts of the country and world who face opposition for proclaiming Christ?

Part III: Personal Application and Growth

Today's lesson points to several important truths that apply to our personal lives. Allow these truths to penetrate your mind, soften your heart, deepen your faith and affect your behavior to help you continually grow in Christ.

1. We should put love into action to encourage one another in faith.

Consider various opportunities to volunteer in missions, prison ministry, a Christian pregnancy resource center, promotion of financial stewardship in your church, intercessory prayer for persecuted pastors, etc. Starting this week, in what way will you regularly participate in one of these opportunities so as to personally encourage fellow believers?

2. Our personal behavior affects the entire body of Christ, the church.

Who will you ask today to be your ongoing accountability partner in connection with a specific area of temptation where you struggle to remain faithful, such as pornography or a weak prayer life? What benefit do you anticipate as a result of allowing someone to encourage you? Who will you encourage in turn?

3. We are to pray for and support our church leaders.

Each Sunday bless your pastor by asking, "How can I be praying for you?" Set aside a regular time each week to pray by name for your pastors, church officers, and their families. If you do not know your church leaders, when will you introduce yourself to them so you have a more personal connection?

Part IV: Closing Devotion
by Charles Spurgeon

Believer, you are invited to come and dine with Jesus under the banner of redeeming love. It is an invitation to nearness to Jesus. It is also an invitation to enjoy fellowship with the saints. Christians may differ on a variety of points, but they all have one spiritual appetite; and even if we cannot all *feel* in agreement, we can all *feed* in agreement on the bread of life sent down from heaven.

At the table of fellowship with Jesus we are one. Get nearer to Jesus, and you will find yourself linked more and more in spirit to all who are like yourself, supported by the same heavenly manna. If we draw nearer to Jesus we shall be nearer to one another.

To look at Christ is to live, but for strength to serve Him you must come and dine. We labor under much unnecessary weakness on account of neglecting this precept. Thus, if you want to realize nearness to Jesus, union with Jesus, strength from Jesus, and love for His people, come and dine with Him by faith.[91]

⮾ Lesson 24 ⮿

Benediction

Hebrews 13:20-25

Part I: Setting the Stage

Purpose

This lesson brings our study of Hebrews to a close. Hebrews ends with a stirring benediction packed with theological truths that encourage us to keep the faith, followed by a few personal greetings from the author. It is important for us to trust that God equips us to do His will and that He makes it possible for us to persevere in our faith in Christ.

Look for the following application points in this lesson:

1. We are at peace with God through Jesus Christ.
2. God equips us with everything good to do His will and please Him.
3. Today is the best time to strengthen our faith and grow in spiritual maturity.

Reaching the End

We have come to the closing verses of Hebrews and it should be no surprise that the book's ending is just as profound as its beginning. The author has maintained an intense pace all along and we are the richer for it.

You will find that the benediction mentions several things for the first time. These were alluded to earlier but are now specifically stated: God is a God of peace, God raised Jesus from the dead, Jesus is the great shepherd, and the new covenant is an eternal covenant.

Think of the opening paragraph of Hebrews and its emphasis on the majesty and power of God and Christ. Hebrews closes with an emphasis on what Christ's majesty and power have done for us: we are at peace with God, death has been conquered by Christ, and we will enjoy the blessings of the new covenant forever. Here is solid reassurance that God equips us with every good thing and works in us so we may do His will and please Him forever.

Truly, Amen

In some manuscripts the benediction closes with the Hebrew word *amen*, meaning truly, verily, or so be it. This is strong affirmation of the truth of what was said, and an expression of sure hope of its fulfillment by God. When Jesus prefaced His sayings with *amen* He stressed the truth and validity of His word.

The Bible consistently conveys the view that there is real, knowable truth. Our society's post-modern assertion that there is no ultimate truth is foreign to Scripture's thinking and to most of human history. The Bible adheres to the correspondence theory of truth in which truth corresponds to reality, as God sees it. Truth is what is really real and true.

Here we see the dilemma that arises when post-modern thinkers approach the Bible. They read it with a presupposition that it must be opinion because they have been taught that truth is relative, cannot be known, or there is no truth out there to know. This line of reasoning is self-defeating, though, for it is inevitably stated as if it were absolutely true. A consistent post-modern view is ultimately meaningless and unlivable.

We must approach the Bible with a heart for truth. The Bible sets forth truth for our everlasting benefit. We can question it, but in the end we, like the apostle Thomas, are to acknowledge the truth. Jesus told Thomas, "I am the way, and the truth, and the life. No one comes to the Father except through me." (John 14:6)

Finishing Well

Christians are called to finish well by persevering in faith to the end of life. None of us knows how long our lives will be or when Christ will return, so today is always the best time to take steps toward becoming more mature in faith. Strong and mature faith gives us assurance of salvation and helps us pass along the faith, face persecution, deal with aging, and prepare for eternity with God. The closing benediction of Hebrews reminds us that God is the one who makes it possible for us to finish well by means of His power and the love and saving work of Jesus Christ. What a great encouragement to keep the faith.

Part II: Studying Scripture

Read Hebrews 13:20-21

In many churches the pastor pronounces a benediction at the end of the worship service to invoke God's blessing on the congregation. Hebrews 13:20-21 is a favorite benediction.

1. The God of Peace and Resurrection

Hebrews 1 opened with an emphasis on God the Creator and King of the universe, but now the author calls Him the God of peace. God is at peace with us only because Jesus made atonement for our sins. Jesus bore God's wrath and intercedes for us in heaven so we might know God as a God of peace to whom we can draw near without fear of condemnation.

a) What does it mean to you to know that the God who is at peace with us is the one who equips us to do His will?

b) Read Numbers 6:24-26, the familiar Aaronic benediction. What theme(s) do you find in common with the Hebrews 13 benediction?

c) God brought Jesus back from the dead by the blood of the new covenant. In v. 20, why do you think the author chooses this context to refer to Jesus as the great shepherd of the sheep? What is any great shepherd willing to do to protect the sheep? (See John 10:11-15)

d) No one else has been brought back to life forever like Jesus. His resurrection was a profound miracle that proved the truth of who He said He was. Describe the kind of power you imagine the resurrection required.

2. Equipped to Persevere

a) The first verse of the benediction (v. 20) tells what God has done in Christ. The second verse (v. 21) tells what God is doing in Christ's people. The author employs a literary couplet in v. 21 to emphasize the significance of what he is saying by repeating it with slightly different words:

God equips us with every good work. Why? _____

God works in us. What is the result? _____

b) The word "equip" in Greek literally means to restore, mend, or make complete. God restores believers to wholeness and enables them to obey His will. This is one of the blessings of the new covenant of grace. How does it make you feel to know that the same immense power that raised Jesus also restores and equips us to do God's will?

c) Everything comes together at this point. This is why we can have confidence that we will persevere in faith despite persecution, doubts, ridicule, and other obstacles in our path: it is God who perseveres to bring us to glory. We do not have to do this on our own and in fact we cannot do it on our own. God will equip us. What is your response to this good news?

3.   Glory Forever and Ever, Amen

a)   The benediction ends, "to whom be glory forever and ever, amen." The original Greek is not clear as to whether the glory goes to God or Christ. The sentence structure favors Christ, but both readings are found elsewhere in Scripture. Why is it relatively unimportant to settle the question of whether the author means that our glory goes to God the Father or God the Son?

b)   Theologian R. B. Kuiper exhorts us to live every moment for God's glory:

> "Not only does the church glorify God in its services of worship, but through those services its members are stimulated to do all their living to God's glory – to serve God not merely on the Lord's Day, but all the days of the week; not merely in God's house, but also in their homes; not merely on the day of rest, but also in their daily work; not merely when partaking of the holy supper, but also when eating their daily bread; not merely when singing psalms and hymns and spiritual songs, but also when listening to the symphonies of Brahms; not merely when praying, but also when playing."[92]

In what ordinary area of life will you endeavor to give God more glory?

c)   The final word of the benediction is *amen* (ah-MANE), Hebrew for "truly." The author asserts the truth of what he says. Why is *amen* an appropriate ending?

d) Author Nancy Pearcey confirms that truth is knowable and corresponds to historical reality:

> "The central claim of Christianity is a stubborn historical fact, which was open to empirical investigation and knowable by ordinary means of historical verification... The key to the power of the biblical message is the conviction that it is actually true – objectively, universally, cosmically true."[93]

Why is it essential to our faith that the resurrection is a real historical event?

Read Hebrews 13:22-25

4. Greetings

a) In v. 22, the author says he has written a brief or short letter of few words. The letter itself takes only an hour to read, but it can fill a lifetime of study. Which parts of Hebrews do you wish the author had explained more fully?

b) In v. 23, Timothy is probably the same person as the co-worker of the apostle Paul. Evidently Timothy had been imprisoned and released. What does the author hope Timothy will be available to do?

c) In v. 24, "Greet all your leaders and all the saints" suggests the letter was intended to circulate among house churches known to the author. If you had been a 1st century believer hearing this letter read out loud at one sitting, and you knew the author, what would have been your reaction?

d) In v. 24, the author sends greetings on behalf of "those from Italy." As mentioned in Lesson 1, it is not known who these Italians were. Since the letter began without a greeting, how does this closing make the letter more personal?

5. Grace

a) The author finishes with a typical blessing, "Grace be with all of you." Grace is the distinguishing feature of the new covenant in Christ and involves elements of God's love, forgiveness, and empowerment to obey. A traditional definition of grace is "God's unmerited favor." Explain this definition in your own words.

b) Why should believers be eager to speak words of grace to each other?

c) What tone does the mention of grace lend to the whole letter of Hebrews?

d) Ministry leader Joni Eareckson Tada has been a quadriplegic for forty-six years and has also dealt with serious illness. She understands the need for grace on a daily basis:

> "Oh, friend, God could have set up a throne of strict justice, dispensing death to all who were convened before it; oh no, but God has, instead, chosen to set up a throne of grace. What an encouragement that is to us sinners! There, at that throne, grace reigns, and acts with sovereign freedom, power and bounty...

"And it is this amazing grace that I thrive on; I flourish on grace; I prosper spiritually on God's grace, and I learned to lean on it early in my paralysis. I couldn't live without it, or more accurately, I could not live without the Lord of grace, Jesus Himself... When God gives us grace, He gives us the Lord of grace, Jesus. Yes, the throne of grace really is that personal."[94]

How will you allow God's grace to transform your suffering and struggles so you can joyfully say you know the Lord of grace in this personal way?

6. Bringing Our Study to an End

a) As this study comes to a close, what three words would you use to describe the book of Hebrews? What three words describe its effect on you?

b) Take an hour as soon as possible to re-read the entire book of Hebrews at one sitting. You might want to listen to an audio version. As you come across themes or passages you would like to explore further, make a plan to pursue them.

Part III: Personal Application and Growth

Today's lesson points to several important truths that apply to our personal lives. Allow these truths to penetrate your mind, soften your heart, deepen your faith and affect your behavior to help you continually grow in Christ.

1. We are at peace with God through Jesus Christ.

The benediction is a mini-gospel that reminds us we are saved from God's wrath through the work of Jesus Christ. This week repeat the benediction often with the goal of committing it to memory for your own encouragement:

> "Now may the God of peace who brought again from the dead our Lord Jesus, the great shepherd of the sheep, by the blood of the eternal covenant, equip you with everything good that you may do his will, working in us that which is pleasing in his sight, through Jesus Christ, to whom be glory forever and ever. Amen." (Hebrews 13:20-21)

2. God equips us with everything good to do His will and please Him.

What will you do differently this week to demonstrate your awareness that God is the one, not you, who powerfully and perfectly equips you to do His will?

3. Today is the best time to strengthen our faith and grow in spiritual maturity.

The last six chapters of Hebrews encourage us to keep the faith through a deeper understanding of Christ's priesthood, inspiration by heroes of the faith, personal hope, and practical expressions of love for the body of Christ. Take a look at the application points at the ends of Lessons 13-24 (see the complete list in Appendix A). Note several points that were new to you or personally meaningful. In what ways have you been encouraged to keep the faith as a result of studying the second half of Hebrews? How will you use the complete list of application points as a tool to further your growth in spiritual maturity?

Congratulations on finishing this study! Ask the Holy Spirit to continue to apply God's word to your heart and mind so that the insights you have gained will be a lasting blessing to you and others.

Part IV: Closing Devotion

by Charles Spurgeon

Believer, Heaven will be full of ceaseless praises to Jesus Christ!

Is He not a Priest forever after the order of Melchizedek?
> To Him be glory forever!
Is He not King forever, King of kings and Lord of lords?
> To Him be glory forever!

You are eagerly anticipating the time when you shall join the saints above in ascribing all glory to Jesus, but are you glorifying Him *now*?

Dear Lord,
Help me to glorify You.
I am poor: help me to glorify You by contentment;
I am sick: help me to give You honor by patience;
I have talents: help me to extol You by spending them for You;
I have time: help me to redeem it, that I may serve You;
I have a head to think: help me to think of You;
I have a heart to feel: let my heart feel Your love and glow with affection for
> *You.*

You have put me in this world for something; Lord, show me what that is, and help me to work out my life-purpose. I cannot do much, but as the widow put in her two small coins, which were all her living, so, Lord, I cast my time and eternity too into Your treasury. I am all Yours. Take me, and enable me to glorify You now, in all that I say, in all that I do, and with all that I have.

Amen.[95]

❧ Appendix A ❦
Application Points

A list of the personal application points at the end of each lesson.

SECTION I: THE PERSON OF JESUS CHRIST (WHO HE IS)

<u>Lesson 1</u> Christ's Divinity: The Son of God
The Son of God is fully divine, God Himself.
The Son of God is the second person of the Trinity.
Jesus Christ is the Son of God, fully divine, fully God.

<u>Lesson 2</u> Christ's Divinity: The Messiah
Jesus is the promised Messiah, the Son of God, God Himself.
Jesus is superior to angels and enthroned at God's right hand.
Angels are created spirit beings who, like us, worship God the Son, Jesus
      Christ.

<u>Lesson 3</u> Jesus' Humanity: Our Savior
Jesus Christ is fully human, God incarnate.
Jesus restored humanity's divinely ordained role as ruler of creation.
Jesus had to suffer and die in our place in order to be our Savior.

<u>Lesson 4</u> Jesus' Humanity: Our Brother
Jesus suffered temptation and will help us when we are tempted.
Jesus is our sympathetic high priest when we fail to resist temptation.
Believers are spiritual brothers and sisters to Jesus and to each other.

SECTION II: THE WORK OF JESUS CHRIST (WHAT HE HAS DONE)

<u>Lesson 5</u> The Greatest Prophet
Jesus perfectly fulfills the office of prophet by mediating God's plan of
      salvation.

There is only one people of God, the true church, made up of believers
   from all eras.
Those belonging to God's household remain faithful to Christ to the end.

Lesson 6 Revealing God's Saving Word
Christians belong to God's household and willingly obey His rules.
People should respond in belief to God's saving word.
Those that permanently reject Jesus Christ will never have salvation.

Lesson 7 Revealing God's Eternal Rest
Entering God's rest means enjoying fellowship with God due to Christ's
   atonement.
Believers enter God's rest now and forever by faith in Jesus Christ.
We must put our faith in Christ while there is still time.

Lesson 8 The Greatest Priest
Jesus perfectly fulfills the office of high priest by His sacrifice and
   intercession.
Believers pray to God through Jesus Christ, their eternal high priest.
We should join in Christ's work of intercession by praying for others.

Lesson 9 Attention! Seek Mature Teaching
Believers can strengthen their faith by studying mature Christian teaching.
An ongoing desire to seek mature teaching gives us assurance of salvation.
Rituals and church doctrine are essential companions to our faith life.

Lesson 10 Attention! Believe God's Promises
God's promises to Abraham extend to all true believers, the universal
   church.
We have assurance that God keeps His saving promises.
Our hope of salvation is anchored in heaven where Jesus lives to intercede
   for us.

Lesson 11 The Greatest King
Jesus perfectly fulfills the office of king.
Jesus reigns as a king of righteousness and peace.
It is encouraging to know God provides His people with a royal priesthood.

<u>Lesson 18</u> Benefits of Christ's Sacrifice
Christ's sacrifice makes it possible for us to draw near to God with confidence.
We are to persevere in faith to the end of life.
Believers should encourage one another to keep the faith.

SECTION IV: PRACTICAL EVIDENCE OF OUR SALVATION

<u>Lesson 19</u> Confident Faith
Faith is the assurance of things hoped for, the conviction of things not seen.
We should imitate the confident faith of past believers.
The patriarchs believed God without seeing fulfillment in their lifetimes.

<u>Lesson 20</u> Courageous Faith
We should imitate the courageous faith of past believers.
Jesus Christ is the fulfillment of God's saving promises.
Old and New Testament believers together form one people of God.

<u>Lesson 21</u> Enduring Hope
We are to put our hope in Jesus Christ.
Suffering can be a means of discipline to help us grow toward spiritual
    maturity.
Christians are meant to finish the race of life well, persevering in faith to
    the end.

<u>Lesson 22</u> Unshakable Hope
The old covenant of law pointed to death; the new covenant of grace points
    to life.
Our hope of salvation is unshakable because Christ's kingdom is unshakable.
We should respond to God with reverent worship.

<u>Lesson 23</u> Brotherly Love
We should put love into action to encourage one another in faith.
Our personal behavior affects the entire body of Christ, the church.
We are to pray for and support our church leaders.

<u>Lesson 24</u> Benediction
We are at peace with God through Jesus Christ.
God equips us with everything good to do His will and please Him.
Today is the best time to strengthen our faith and grow in spiritual maturity.

❧ Appendix B ❧
Leader's Guide

This leader's guide is intended to help you get the most out of your group study of *Looking to Christ: The Book of Hebrews.* Whether one person leads all the lessons or the leadership is passed around, it is hoped that this guide will encourage and equip the leader to present the lessons in a way that meets the needs of individuals and the group as a whole.

The Goal of Bible Study
The overall goal of Bible study is for lives to be transformed through the power of God's word applied by the Holy Spirit. Studying Scripture should change one's mind, heart and behavior for Christ. Encourage participants to engage their emotions and cognitive thinking as they study, and put the truths of Scripture into practice in their personal lives.

Overall Planning
There are 24 lessons in this study. Each lesson is designed to take about an hour for group discussion, plus you will want to provide additional time for announcements, prayer concerns, and fellowship. You should feel free to make adjustments to cover the material in a way that fits your group's particular schedule and interest.

Homework for Participants
Everyone will get more out of the Scripture and lessons if they answer the study questions ahead of time, including the first lesson. Encourage participants to set aside time to do the homework. Thoughtful preparation will allow participants to follow the group discussion better, and they will be more ready for deeper levels of insight.

The reality, of course, is that most people are pressed for time. Not everyone will be able to fully prepare ahead of time. By all means be gracious to them.

They will be blessed by participating in the group even if it is the first time they have read the material.

Leader Preparation
The leader should do the same homework as the participants. In addition, there are a couple of things the leader will want to do to be better prepared:

- Pray for participants by name during the week. Lift up their individual concerns to the Lord and pray that each person will find time to study.
- Glance at the Endnotes to see if there is additional background information for the lesson that will be helpful.

Appreciating Differences
A good leader will remember that people approach a Bible study text with different expectations influenced by their style of learning:[96]

Imaginative learners want to see the big picture and know why the information is important before they get started.
Analytic learners like lots of facts and details and enjoy learning information for its own sake.
Common sense learners solve problems and want to put the information to practical use.
Dynamic learners are creative and want to find ways to apply the information in their personal life.

Keep in mind that people also have different learning modes. Your preferred mode may or may not match others in the group. For instance, visual learners tend to like maps and auditory learners may appreciate poetry.

People take part in Bible study groups for a number of valid reasons. Some people hunger to know God's word more deeply or need a safe place to ask hard spiritual questions, while others long for comforting fellowship and intercessory prayer. Some may just be curious.

Ask the Lord to help you be compassionate and sensitive to the wide range of learning styles, modes, motivations, and needs among your group.

Leading the Lesson
Start with a prayer asking the Holy Spirit to enlighten your hearts and minds with the truth of Scripture and apply it to your lives.

Part I: Setting the Stage
Read the opening pages out loud. These remarks tell what the lesson is about, why it is important, and relevant background material. Imaginative learners will benefit from knowing the big picture of the lesson up front.

Part II: Studying Scripture
Ask a volunteer to read the Scripture passage out loud. Do not press someone to read in front of others if they are not comfortable. Be kind and supportive if someone gets a passage with names that are difficult to pronounce.

Read each study question out loud and invite answers. Most of your time will be spent on these questions. The leader should not be the first to answer the study questions and should not even add further comments if the group's answers are sufficient. Watch the time and try not to let anyone dominate the discussion. Analytic learners will especially enjoy this part of the lesson with its emphasis on facts and interpretation of Scripture.

Part III: Personal Application and Growth
Read each application point out loud and invite answers to the questions. If a point is too personal, allow people to reflect silently on their commitment to change. Ask if anyone wants to offer additional points of application.

Dynamic and common sense learners will welcome the chance to apply the lesson in practical ways in the coming week. All learning styles will benefit from questions that challenge them to envision the way their faith will mature as a result of applying the lesson.

Part IV: Closing Devotion
Read Spurgeon's devotion out loud and close with a brief prayer of your own.

✎ Appendix C ✎
About Hermeneutics

"Then we will no longer be infants, tossed back and forth by the waves,
and blown here and there by every wind of teaching…"
(Ephesians 4:14)

Certain principles guide our study of the Bible so that we remain faithful to the Biblical text. We do not want to get lost in unfounded speculation. It is considered good procedure when police detectives follow established guidelines during investigations so they do not overlook evidence or draw wrong conclusions. Similarly, we will follow established guidelines for Bible study. These guidelines belong to the field of hermeneutics (her-men-OO-ticks).

Everyone studies the Bible with a hermeneutic, a set of interpretive principles. Even people who have never heard of the word can appreciate that the way they interpret a passage is influenced by their understanding of history, grammar, and logic. One thing that can make Bible study perplexing, though, is that there is no definitive hermeneutic with which everyone agrees. That means different scholars might come up with different interpretations of a passage depending on which interpretive principles they apply.

The choice of interpretive principles is extremely important since a faulty hermeneutic can lead even well-meaning people to misguided conclusions. Evangelical scholars generally adhere to certain traditional rules of interpretation based on Reformation principles covering four areas: historical, cultural, theological, and literary. This is the grammatico-historical approach. It is designed to discover the author's original intended meaning by looking at the background, context, theology, and grammatical features.

The following list gives a few of the principles this study is based on. A good study Bible like *The Reformation Study Bible (ESV)* can provide some of the background, language analysis, and commentary suggested below.

255

Seven Principles of Interpretation

1. Consider the historical setting.
Study the period of history in which the incident occurred or was recorded. Learn about the rulers of the day, natural disasters, and major events. For example, look at New Testament events in the context of the Roman Empire.

2. Study the cultural setting.
Learn about the customs, food, clothing, religion, geography, and economics of the time. Consider the national and racial backgrounds of the people involved.

3. Read the Scriptural context.
Read the immediate context consisting of the paragraph and chapter in which the verse is located. Then look at the broader context of the whole book, other books by the same author, and the entire Bible.

4. Appreciate the unity of the Old and New Testaments.
When reading a New Testament text, discover whether it alludes to the Old Testament and what its connection teaches us. When reading the Old Testament, ask what the passage teaches about God's redemptive purposes which are ultimately fulfilled in Jesus Christ.

5. Let Scripture interpret Scripture ("the analogy of faith").
Interpret a difficult passage in light of related, clear passages. Read the clear passages first and then read the difficult one in light of their meaning.

6. Read the Bible in a literary way (*sensus literalis*).
Identify the literary genre of the passage (poetry, narrative, letter, etc.). Look for metaphors and literary structure. Remember that poetry, prophecy, and apocalyptic are not meant to be read in a consistently literal way.

7. Go back to the original languages (*ad fontes,* "to the source").
Study a translation of the Bible rather than a paraphrased version. The Old Testament was written mostly in Hebrew and the New Testament in Greek.

❧ Select Bibliography ❧

Apologetics
Bahnsen, Greg L. *Always Ready.* Nacogdoches, TX: Covenant Media Press, 1996.

Keller, Timothy. *The Reason for God: Belief in an Age of Skepticism.* New York: Dutton, 2008.

Packer, J. I. *Knowing God.* Downers Grove, IL: InterVarsity Press, 1973.

Pearcey, Nancy. *Saving Leonardo: A Call to Resist the Secular Assault on Mind, Morals, & Meaning.* Nashville: B & H Publishing Group, 2010.

Schaefer, Francis A. *The God Who Is There.* Downers Grove, IL: InterVarsity Press, 1982.

Sproul, R. C. *Defending Your Faith: An Introduction to Apologetics.* Wheaton, IL: Crossway Books, 2003; http://www.ligonier.org/store.

Strobel, Lee. *The Case for Christ: A Journalist's Personal Investigation of the Evidence for Jesus.* Grand Rapids, MI: Zondervan, 1998.

Commentaries
Bruce, F.F. *The Epistle to the Hebrews.* The New International Commentary on the New Testament. Grand Rapids, MI: William B. Eerdmans Publishing Company, 1990.

Guthrie, Donald. *The Letter to the Hebrews.* The Tyndale New Testament Commentaries. Grand Rapids, MI: William B. Eerdmans Publishing Company, 1983.

Hendriksen, William and Simon J. Kistemaker. "Hebrews." *New Testament Commentary: Thessalonians, the Pastorals, and Hebrews*. Grand Rapids, MI: Baker Academic, 1984.

Leading a Bible Study
Bennett, Dennis. "How We Teach and How They Learn." *Equip to Disciple*. Series of ten articles. Lawrenceville, GA: Presbyterian Church in America, 2009-2011. Read at http://www.equip.pcacep.org/search.

Nielson, Kathleen Buswell. *Bible Study: Following the Ways of the Word*. Phillipsburg, NJ: P & R Publishing Company, 2011.

Persecution
Annual Global Report on the Church. Voice of the Martyrs, Inc., 2014. Available at https://www.persecution.com.

Wurmbrand, Richard. *Tortured for Christ*. Bartlesville, OK: Living Sacrifice Book Company, 1967, 1998.

Reference books
Beale, G.K. and D. A. Carson. *Commentary on the New Testament Use of the Old Testament*. Grand Rapids, MI: Baker Academic, 2007.

Berkhof, Louis. *Systematic Theology*. Grand Rapids, MI: William B. Eerdmans Publishing Company, 1996.

Frame, John M. *The Doctrine of God*. Phillipsburg, NJ: P & R Publishing, 2002.

Grudem, Wayne. *Systematic Theology: An Introduction to Biblical Doctrine*. Grand Rapids, MI: Zondervan, 1994.

Sanctification
Chambers, Oswald. *My Utmost for His Highest*. Grand Rapids, MI: Discovery House Publishers, 1963.

Spurgeon, Charles H. *Morning and Evening*. 1865, 1868. Available at http://www.ccel.org/ccel/spurgeon/morneve. Public Domain.

❧ Endnotes ❦

Lesson 1: Christ's Divinity: The Son of God

[1] PART I: Setting the Stage, "Title"

The name of Hebrews for God's people goes back to the time of Abraham through Moses (2000-1500 B.C.). God's people were generally called Israelites from the time of Moses to David (1500-1000 B.C.), and Jews after that. Hebraic Jews in Jesus' time were sometimes called Hebrews to distinguish them from Hellenistic (Greek-speaking) Jews (see Acts 6:1). Perhaps references to Hebrews and the Tabernacle reminded readers that the Levitical worship system set up by Moses was obsolete due to Christ.

[2] Herman Bavinck, *Reformed Dogmatics,* Vol. 2, "God and Creation" (Grand Rapids, MI: Baker Academic, 2004), 333.

[3] PART II: Studying Scripture, Question 3, "The Son of God and the Trinity"

Analogies of the Trinity are always inadequate in some way. The shamrock and egg analogies teach that God is one being with three parts; the problem is that each part is not fully the whole, implying that each person is not fully God. Modalism teaches that God is one person acting in three roles or modes at different times; the problem is that modalism fails to affirm the plurality or distinctness of persons in God.

[4] PART II: Studying Scripture, Question 4a, "The Son's Two Natures"

A low view of Christ's divinity is associated with certain heresies. Moralism is a belief that Jesus was a good moral example as a human, but He was not divine. Arianism is a belief that Jesus was fully human, but not fully divine. Deism is a belief that God is Creator but does not sustain the world, and Jesus is not His divine Son.

[5] PART II: Studying Scripture, Question 4b, "The Son's Two Natures"

A low view of Christ's humanity is associated with certain heresies. Pantheism is a belief that the whole universe is the same thing as God. Gnosticism includes, among other things, belief that the material world is bad and the spiritual world is good, so the divine Christ could not have been truly human.

[6] Abraham Kuyper, "Sphere Sovereignty," *Abraham Kuyper, A Centennial Reader,* James D. Bratt, Ed. (Grand Rapids, MI: Wm. B. Eerdmans Publishing Co., 1998), 488.

[7] Charles H. Spurgeon, *Morning and Evening,* adapted from January 27 Morning; http://www.ccel.org/ccel/spurgeon/morneve; Public Domain.

Lesson 2: Christ's Divinity: The Messiah

[8] Jack W. Hayford, "Majesty, Worship His Majesty" (Rocksmith Music, 1981); http://www.jackhayford.org/pages/majesty.

[9] The Belgic Confession, Article 10, "The Deity of Christ," 1619. *NIV Spirit of the Reformation Study Bible* (Grand Rapids, MI: Zondervan, 2003), 2155.

[10] Charles H. Spurgeon, *Morning and Evening,* adapted from January 9 Evening; http://www.ccel.org/ccel/spurgeon/morneve; Public Domain.

Lesson 3: Jesus' Humanity: Our Savior

[11] Geerhardus Vos, *Biblical Theology* (Carlisle, PA: The Banner of Truth Trust, 1948), 341.

[12] Wayne Grudem, *Systematic Theology* (Grand Rapids, MI: Zondervan, 1994), 543.

[13] Lee Strobel, *The Case for Christ* (Grand Rapids, MI: Zondervan, 1998), 248.

[14] Louis Berkhof, *Systematic Theology* (Grand Rapids, MI: William B. Eerdmans Publishing Company, 1996), 332-343.

[15] Charles H. Spurgeon, *Morning and Evening,* adapted from March 30 Morning; http://www.ccel.org/ccel/spurgeon/morneve; Public Domain.

Lesson 4: Jesus' Humanity: Our Brother

[16] PART I: Setting the Stage, "Facing Temptation"
Jesus' three wilderness temptations were reminders of the Israelites' temptations. (1) Discontentment: The hungry Israelites complained about God's provision (Ex. 16:3); Jesus was hungry but refused to turn stones into bread, trusting that God could provide manna if needed (Luke 4:4 from Deut. 8:3). (2) Idolatry: The Israelites sought prosperity by worshiping other gods (Ex. 32:8; Num. 25:1-3); Jesus refused to gain kingdoms by worshiping Satan (Luke 4:8 from Deut. 6:13). (3) Unbelief: The Israelites did not trust God to keep His promise to save them (Ex. 17:7); Jesus refused to jump off the Temple to force God to prove He would save (Luke 4:12 from Deut. 6:16).

[17] John M. Frame, *The Doctrine of God* (Phillipsburg, NJ: P & R Publishing, 2002), 678.

[18] John Piper, *Fifty Reasons Why Jesus Came to Die* (formerly published as *The Passion of Jesus Christ*) (Wheaton, IL: Crossway, 2006), 51, 73.

[19] Charles H. Spurgeon, Morning *and Evening*, adapted from January 23 Morning; http://www.ccel.org/ccel/spurgeon/morneve; Public Domain.

Lesson 5: The Greatest Prophet

[20] John Calvin, *Institutes of the Christian Religion*, Book II.15.1; http://www.ccel.org/calvin/institutes.iv.xvi; Public Domain.

[21] Barry C. Black, *From the Hood to the Hill: A Story of Overcoming* (Nashville, TN: Thomas Nelson, 2006), xii. Reprinted by permission. All rights reserved.

[22] Charles H. Spurgeon, *Morning and Evening*, adapted from May 26 Evening; http://www.ccel.org/ccel/spurgeon/morneve; Public Domain.

Lesson 6: Revealing God's Saving Word

[23] S. Truett Cathy, *Eat Mor Chikin*®: Inspire More People (Decatur, GA: Looking Glass Books, 2002), 172.

[24] Charles H. Spurgeon, *Morning and Evening*, adapted from August 15 Evening; http://www.ccel.org/ccel/spurgeon/morneve; Public Domain.

Lesson 7: Revealing God's Eternal Rest

[25] PART I: Setting the Stage, "Entering God's Rest"
The author of Hebrews does not mention the weekly Sabbath rest (*sabbaton*), but the weekly observance is encoded in the Ten Commandments, God's moral law which is still in effect today. Keeping the Sabbath holy is the fourth commandment. Scripture gives two related, authoritative reasons for observing the Sabbath: God's revelation in Creation (Ex. 31:16-17) and God's redemption in the Exodus (Deut. 5:12-15).

[26] Saint Augustine, *Confessions*, Book I.l; http://www.ccel.org/ccel/augustine/confess.ii.i; Public Domain.

[27] John Adams and John Quincy Adams, *The Selected Writings of John and John Quincy Adams*, Adrienne Koch and William Peden, Eds. (New York: Alfred A. Knopf, 1946), 292; Letter of January 3, 1817.

[28] Charles H. Spurgeon, *Morning and Evening*, adapted from October 2 Morning; http://www.ccel.org/ccel/spurgeon/morneve; Public Domain.

Lesson 8: The Greatest Priest

[29] Louis Berkhof, *Systematic Theology*, 403-405.

[30] Hywel R. Jones, *Let's Study Hebrews* (Carlisle, PA: The Banner of Truth Trust, 2002), 27.

[31] Oswald Chambers, *My Utmost for His Highest* (©1935 by Dodd Mead & Co., renewed ©1963 by the Oswald Chambers Publications Assn., Ltd.), 125, 65. Used by permission of Discovery House Publishers, Grand Rapids, MI 49501. All rights reserved.

[32] John Murray, *Redemption Accomplished and Applied* (Grand Rapids, MI: Wm. B. Eerdmans Publishing Company, 1955), 28.

[33] Charles H. Spurgeon, *Morning and Evening,* adapted from January 11 Evening; http://www.ccel.org/ccel/spurgeon/morneve; Public Domain.

Lesson 9: Attention! Seek Mature Teaching
[34] Blaise Pascal, *Pensées,* Section VIII, "The Fundamentals of the Christian Religion," No. 556 (first published 1670); http://www.ccel.org/ccel/pascal/pensees.ix.html; Public Domain.

[35] PART II: Studying Scripture, Question 3b, "Confident Faith"
The author lists six foundational teachings he expects the readers to know:
(1) Repentance from dead works: This refers either to deeds that incur the death penalty or the futile effort to earn salvation by our works. (2) Faith: We are to believe God's character, word, and saving acts in Christ. (3) Instruction about washings (literally "baptisms"): There is only one Christian baptism (Eph. 4:5) but the term might include the baptism of repentance offered by John the Baptist. It might instead refer to Jewish priestly ceremonial washings that foreshadowed Christ's cleansing work. (4) The laying on of hands: This might refer to healings, ordination, blessings, and the gift of the Holy Spirit in baptism. (5) The resurrection of the dead: Everyone will be bodily resurrected at the end times; believers live eternally in heaven and unbelievers in hell. (6) Eternal judgment: Unbelievers will be sentenced to eternal punishment in hell.

[36] PART II: Studying Scripture, Question 4b, "Unbelievers Fall Away"
The participles describing people who fell away are not technical terms and do not imply salvation or regeneration. Jesus said not everyone who professes faith or performs miracles in His name will enter the kingdom of heaven (Matt. 7:21-23). (1) Enlightened *(photizo)* means knowledge in general; it may also refer to baptism. The author uses it to mean knowledge elsewhere in Hebrews. People who were enlightened understood the truth of the gospel but may not have had saving faith. (2) Tasted *(geuomai)* means to know something by experience, but not accept it in full measure. Those who tasted heard the gospel and witnessed the power of the Spirit.

(3) Shared (literally, "became partakers," *metochos*) means to associate with someone. It could imply close attachment with saving results or loose attachment with no transformation. The author uses the word both ways elsewhere in Hebrews.

[37] PART II: Studying Scripture, Question 4e, "Unbelievers Fall Away"
Jesus held Judas Iscariot fully responsible for his wickedness (John 6:65; Matt. 26:24). Judas was not among God's elect, but he did not have to betray Jesus. All people, whether elect or not, are obligated to act as responsible human agents in accord with the moral code and knowledge of God inherent in them (Rom. 1:18-21). The apostle Paul reminds us not to judge God's election as unfair (Rom. 9:14-24).

[38] PART II: Studying Scripture, Question 4f, "Unbelievers Fall Away"
Repentance has a range of meanings. Outward repentance involves sorrow for sin and perhaps a change in external behavior, but not a transformed heart. Saving repentance not only involves heartfelt sorrow for sin, but also turning in a new direction and resolving to live under Christ's lordship.

[39] PART III: Personal Application and Growth, Question 3
See James Dodds, "Exposition of the Apostles' Creed," 1896; Center for Reformed Theology and Apologetics; http://www.reformed.org/documents; Public Domain.

Twelve Articles of the Apostles' Creed:
(1) I believe in God the Father Almighty, Maker of heaven and earth,
(2) And in Jesus Christ his only Son our Lord,
(3) Who was conceived by the Holy Spirit, born of the Virgin Mary,
(4) Suffered under Pontius Pilate, was crucified, dead, and buried;
(5) He descended into hell; the third day he rose again from the dead;
(6) He ascended into heaven, and sits on the right hand of God the Father Almighty;
(7) From thence he shall come to judge the living and the dead.
(8) I believe in the Holy Spirit;
(9) The holy catholic (universal) church; the communion of saints;
(10) The forgiveness of sins;
(11) The resurrection of the body;
(12) And the life everlasting. Amen.

[40] Charles H. Spurgeon, *Morning and Evening*; adapted from July 26 Morning; http://www.ccel.org/ccel/spurgeon/morneve; Public Domain.

Lesson 10: Attention! Believe God's Promises
[41] Wayne Grudem, *Systematic Theology*, 515.

[42] J. I. Packer, *Knowing God* (Downers Grove, IL: InterVarsity Press, 1973), 217.

[43] Charles H. Spurgeon, *Morning and Evening,* adapted from July 8 Morning; http://www.ccel.org/ccel/spurgeon/morneve; Public Domain.

Lesson 11: The Greatest King

[44] R. C. Sproul, "An Historic Faith," *Tabletalk Magazine,* February 1, 2006; from Ligonier Ministries and R. C. Sproul, ©*Tabletalk* magazine; website: www.ligonier. org/tabletalk; email: tabletalk@ligonier.org; toll free phone: 1-800-435-4343.

[45] Charles H. Spurgeon, *Morning and Evening,* adapted from April 22 Morning; http://www.ccel.org/ccel/spurgeon/morneve; Public Domain.

Lesson 12: A King-Priest Forever

[46] R. C. Sproul, *Reason to Believe* (Grand Rapids, MI: Zondervan Publishing House, 1978), 42-43.

[47] John Murray, *Collected Writings of John Murray,* Vol. 2, "Systematic Theology" (Carlisle, PA: The Banner of Truth Trust, 1977), 274.

[48] Charles H. Spurgeon, *Morning and Evening,* adapted from June 16 Morning; http://www.ccel.org/ccel/spurgeon/morneve; Public Domain. Spurgeon quotes a hymn verse from "An Ode to Sovereign Grace," by Christopher Ness, 1700.

Lesson 13: Mediator of the New Covenant

[49] Wayne Grudem, *Systematic Theology,* 515.

[50] Blaise Pascal, *Pensées,* Section VII, "Morality and Doctrine," No. 547.

[51] Charitie Lees Bancroft, "The Advocate," 1863; http://en.wikipedia.org/wiki/ charitie_lees_bancroft; Public Domain. This hymn has been put to a newer tune, "Before the Throne of God Above," by Vikki Cook of Sovereign Grace Ministries, 1997.

[52] Charles H. Spurgeon, *Morning and Evening,* adapted from December 26 Morning; http://www.ccel.org/ccel/spurgeon/morneve; Public Domain.

Lesson 14: Superiority of the New Covenant

[53] PART I: Setting the Stage, "The Abrahamic Covenant"
Seven major covenants in the Bible are commonly recognized:
(1) Covenant of Works between God and Adam, with Adam as the representative head of humanity; (2) Covenant of Grace between God and believers, with Christ as the representative head of redeemed humanity; (3) Noahic Covenant; (4) Abrahamic Covenant; (5) Mosaic Covenant; (6) Davidic Covenant; and (7) the New Covenant.

[54] PART I: Setting the Stage, "The Abrahamic Covenant"
Reformed theology sees the church as the continuation of the true Israel (Rom. 9:6-8). There is one eternal people of God, the universal church, consisting of believing Jews and Gentiles from all eras (Rom. 11:11-24). The church is the body of Christ and is fulfilling the new covenant in His name (II Cor. 3:5-6).

[55] C. S. Lewis, "A Slip of the Tongue," *The Weight of Glory* (New York: HarperCollins Publishers, Inc., 1976), 190-1. ©C. S. Lewis Pte., Ltd., 1949.

[56] Charles H. Spurgeon, *Morning and Evening,* adapted from August 26 Morning; http://www.ccel.org/ccel/spurgeon/morneve; Public Domain.

Lesson 15: The Sanctuary on Earth

[57] R. C. Sproul, *Now, That's a Good Question* (Wheaton, IL: Tyndale House Publishers, Inc., 1996), 16. Used by permission of Tyndale House Publishers, Inc. All rights reserved.

[58] Charles H. Spurgeon, *Morning and Evening,* adapted from August 28 Morning; http://www.ccel.org/ccel/spurgeon/morneve; Public Domain. Spurgeon mentions Gethsemane (Hebrew for "oil press"), the garden on the Mount of Olives where Jesus prayed for His followers and was arrested after the Last Supper.

Lesson 16: The Sanctuary in Heaven

[59] Martin Luther, *Preface to the Letter of St. Paul to the Romans,* 1522; http://www.ccel.org/ccel/luther/prefacetoromans.iii.html; Public Domain.

[60] Randy Alcorn, *Heaven* (Carol Stream, IL: Tyndale House Publishers, Inc., 2004), 53-54. Used by permission of Tyndale House Publishers, Inc. All rights reserved.

[61] Charles H. Spurgeon, *Morning and Evening,* adapted from December 17 Evening; http://www.ccel.org/ccel/spurgeon/morneve; Public Domain.

Lesson 17: Christ's Superior Sacrifice
[62] William Hendricksen and Simon J. Kistemaker, *Thessalonians, the Pastorals, and Hebrews* (Grand Rapids, MI: Baker Academics, 1984), "Hebrews," 280.

[63] F. F. Bruce, *The Epistle to the Hebrews,* NICNT, The New International Commentary on the New Testament (Grand Rapids, MI: William B. Eerdmans Publishing Company, 1990), 245.

[64] Wayne Grudem, *Systematic Theology,* 991-993.

[65] Francis A. Schaeffer, *True Spirituality* (Carol Stream, IL: Tyndale House Publishers, Inc., 1971, 2011), 92. Used by permission of Tyndale House Publishers, Inc. All rights reserved.

[66] Charles H. Spurgeon, *Morning and Evening,* adapted from January 16 Evening; http://www.ccel.org/ccel/spurgeon/morneve; Public Domain.

Lesson 18: Benefits of Christ's Sacrifice

[67] Zoe Erler, "Remember the Prisoner," *ByFaith Online Magazine* (Lawrenceville, GA: Presbyterian Church in America, February 3, 2014); http://byfaithonline. com/remember-the-prisoner. Mark Casson is Director of MNA Metanoia Prison Ministry, Mission to North America, Presbyterian Church in America; http:// pcamna.org/metanoia-ministries.

[68] William Hendricksen and Simon J. Kistemaker, *Thessalonians, the Pastorals, and Hebrews,* 290.

[69] PART II: Studying Scripture, Question 3b, "No Fear of Condemnation"
Regarding an unbeliever who has profaned the blood of the covenant "by which he *was sanctified"* (Heb. 10:29), some commentators take the phrase to mean "by which he *would have been sanctified;"* unbelievers who permanently reject Christ are never sanctified, either in a sense of one-time justification or a process of growing in holiness.

[70] PART II: Studying Scripture, Question 3c, "No Fear of Condemnation"
The passage from Deut. 32:35-36 was the basis of possibly the most famous sermon in American history, "Sinners in the Hands of an Angry God," delivered by Jonathan Edwards during the Great Awakening.

[71] PART II: Studying Scripture, Question 6c, "Perseverance to the End"
The phrase "but the righteous shall live by his faith" (Hab. 2:4) has inspired countless believers. It influenced Paul (Rom. 1:16-17; Gal. 3:11), and his use influenced the Reformers Luther and Calvin. No matter which aspect of the phrase is emphasized (righteousness, living, or faith), salvation is not by our works, but by faith in Christ.

[72] Charles H. Spurgeon, *Morning and Evening,* adapted from January 30 Evening; http://www.ccel.org/ccel/spurgeon/morneve; Public Domain.

Lesson 19: Confident Faith

[73] PART I: Setting the Stage, "The First Major Group: Confident Heroes"
Here are a few references for further study of the heroes mentioned in this lesson: Abel (Gen. 4:3-5); Enoch (Gen. 5:24); Noah (Gen. 6:14-7:7); Abraham (Gen. 12; 22); Sarah (Gen. 21:7); Isaac (Gen. 26-27); Jacob (Gen. 28; 48); Joseph (Gen. 50:24-26).

[74] Jenny the Jewel, "What God Says About Me" (The Christian Broadcasting Network, 2011); http://www.cbn.com/spirituallife/devotions/JennytheJewel.

[75] Charles H. Spurgeon, *Morning and Evening,* adapted from May 2 Evening; http://www.ccel.org/ccel/spurgeon/morneve; Public Domain.

Lesson 20: Courageous Faith

[76] PART I: Setting the Stage, "The Second Major Group: Courageous Heroes"
Here are a few references for further study of the heroes mentioned in this lesson: Moses' parents (Ex. 1:22 – 2:10); Moses (Ex. 2; 12); the Israelites (Ex. 14; Josh. 6); Rahab (Josh. 2; 6); Gideon (Jud. 6:11 - 7:23); Barak (Jud. 4); Samson (Jud. 16:23-30); Jephthah (Jud. 11:1-33); King David (Ps. 51); Samuel (I Sam. 12).

[77] PART II: Studying Scripture, Question 5a, "Victories and Sufferings"
God's faithful judges, kings and prophets experienced various types of victories:

Dominion:	Conquered kingdoms	Joshua; David
	Enforced justice	Samuel
	Obtained promises	Abraham; Joshua
Safety:	Stopped the mouths of lions	Samson; David; Daniel
	Quenched fire	Shadrach; Meshach; Abednego
	Escaped the sword	David; Elijah
Strength:	Strength out of weakness	Samson; Hezekiah
	Mighty in war	David; Othniel; Ehud; Barak
	Put foreign armies to flight	David; Gideon
Resurrection:	Bringing the dead to life	Elijah; Elisha

[78] PART II: Studying Scripture, Question 5f, "After Moses"
God's faithful judges, kings and prophets often experienced opposition:

Suffering:	Torture*	Eleazar
	Mocking, flogging	Michaiah; Jeremiah
	Chains, imprisonment	Michaiah; Jeremiah
Murder:	Stoned	Zechariah
	Sawed in two	Isaiah
	Killed by the sword	Uriah
Poverty:	Destitute, wore animal skins	Elijah; Elisha
	Afflicted, etc.	David; Elijah; prophets hidden by Obadiah

*The Greek word for torture (*tympanum*, Heb. 11:35) is related to the word tympani, a kettledrum. Victims were stretched and beaten, often until death.

[79] Richard Wurmbrand, *Tortured for Christ* (Bartlesville, OK: Living Sacrifice Book Company, 1967, 1998), 88-89. Material used with permission from The Voice of the Martyrs, P.O. Box 443, Bartlesville, OK 74003; phone 1-918-337-8015; website: www.persecution.com.

[80] Charles H. Spurgeon, *Morning and Evening,* adapted from July 9 Morning; http://www.ccel.org/ccel/spurgeon/morneve; Public Domain.

Lesson 21: Enduring Hope
[81] *Westminster Confession of Faith,* "Of the Perseverance of the Saints," XVII.1; http://www.ccel.org/ccel/anonymous/westminster; Public Domain.

[82] Florence May Chadwick; http://en.wikipedia.org/wiki/Florence_May_Chadwick.

[83] Charles H. Spurgeon, *Morning and Evening,* adapted from June 28 Morning; http://www.ccel.org/ccel/spurgeon/morneve; Public Domain.

Lesson 22: Unshakable Hope
[84] PART I: Setting the Stage, "Heaven Later"
Christians hold various views about the timing of Christ's return in relation to His millennial reign in Rev. 20:4. Four major views are amillennialism, post-millennialism, historic premillennialism, and dispensational premillennialism. This study agrees with the amillennial view that the millennium is not a literal future thousand-year period, but the period between Christ's first and second comings; thus we are currently in the millennium of Christ's reign. The kingdom of God has already come (Luke 4:17-21; Matt. 12:28-29) although not yet in full (Matthew 6:10). God's kingdom will be consummated at the end times when Christ returns in glory. For further study see Anthony A. Hoekema, *The Bible and the Future* (Grand Rapids, MI: William B. Eerdmans Publishing Company, 1979).

[85] Author unknown, "An Interview with Francis Collins," *The Question of God* (Tatge/Lasseur Productions, Inc., 2004), WGBH Boston, Public Broadcasting Service; http://www.pbs.org/wgbh/questionofgod/voices/collins.html.

[86] Charles H. Spurgeon, *Morning and Evening,* adapted from June 22 Evening; http://www.ccel.org/ccel/spurgeon/morneve; Public Domain.

Lesson 23: Brotherly Love
[87] William Wrede, quoted by Donald Guthrie, *The Letter to the Hebrews,* The Tyndale New Testament Commentaries (Grand Rapids, MI: William B. Eerdmans Publishing Company, 1983), 267.

[88] *Didache, The Teaching of the Twelve Apostles;* Section 11.4-5; http://www.ccel.org/ccel/richardson/fathers; Public Domain.

[89] Howard Dayton, *Biblical Financial Study* (Gainesville, GA: Crown Financial Ministries, 2003), 163. Website: www.crown.org. Used by permission.

[90] John Calvin, *Commentary on Hebrews;* http://www.ccel.org/ccel/calvin/calcom44; Public Domain.

91 Charles H. Spurgeon, *Morning and Evening,* adapted from October 16 Morning; http://www.ccel.org/ccel/spurgeon/morneve; Public Domain.

Lesson 24: Benediction

92 R. B. Kuiper, *The Glorious Body of Christ* (Carlisle, PA: The Banner of Truth Trust, 1966), 352.

93 Nancy Pearcey, *Saving Leonardo* (Nashville, TN: B & H Publishing Group, 2010), 35. Used by permission.

94 Joni Eareckson Tada, "Before the Throne of God Above," excerpted from Joni and Friends Radio Program #8275 broadcast on January 17, 2014, ©Joni Eareckson Tada. Used by permission of Joni and Friends, PO Box 3333, Agoura Hills, CA 91376. Website: www.joniandfriends.org/radio.

95 Charles H. Spurgeon, *Morning and Evening,* adapted from February 15 Morning; http://www.ccel.org/ccel/spurgeon/morneve; Public Domain.

Appendix B: Leader's Guide

96 Dennis Bennett, "How We Teach and How They Learn," *Equip to Disciple,* Series of ten articles (Lawrenceville, GA: Presbyterian Church in America, 2009-2011); http://www.equip.pcacep.org/search.